OXFORD
INDIA SHORT
INTRODUCTIONS

INDIAN DEMOCRACY

The Oxford India Short
Introductions are concise,
stimulating, and accessible guides
to different aspects of India.
Combining authoritative analysis,
new ideas, and diverse perspectives,
they discuss subjects which are
topical yet enduring, as also
emerging areas of study and debate.

Contents

Preface

It is not easy to write about democracy; it is more difficult to write about democracy in one's own society.
India's democratic enterprise has been quite exciting
and full of possibilities and question marks. This short
introduction to India's democracy is presented at a
time when India is completing seven decades of its free
and democratic existence. Two transformations appear
to stabilize as India completes seventy years of independent and democratic existence. One is the post-
Congress polity. Most analyses of India's democracy
hinge historically on competitive politics dominated by
the Congress party. The interregnum of the past quarter
of a century has now made it clear that not only has the
Congress system been dismantled, the party itself is on
the verge of a terminal collapse. Two, during the same
period of the past quarter of a century, the country has

also gone through a phase of transforming its earlier approach to political economy. That transformation, too, has stabilized by now.

And yet, the juncture at which this book appears is certainly a difficult one. It is necessary for the readers to situate the discussion in the book in the current moment. As this book was being written, three critical questions emerged in the public domain of India. For the first time in the past three decades, India began to experience the overarching dominance of one leader. The relationship between democracy and leadership is dialectical. Leadership is an important feature of democratic politics, and leaders often mediate in extant conflicts and offer acceptable compromises. This is because of the legitimacy enjoyed by leaders in a democracy. At the same time, democracies tend to crave for leaders and then succumb to the authority of the leader. In the rise of Prime Minister Modi's leadership since 2013, India has experienced this dialectical situation. That moment in India's politics appeared at a time when in many parts of the world strong personalities rose to prominence. How India will cope with this trend of personality cult is a critical question of the present moment.

The second critical question that has become pertinent at the present moment is probably even more complicated. A majoritarian version of democracy appears to be settling in India. This trend is distinct from the tendency in democracies to succumb to vagaries of transient *political* majorities. India's majoritarianism tends to challenge its diversity and hurts the majority community as much as it threatens the minority communities because majoritarianism in the Indian context homogenizes the majority religious community. Chapter 6 discusses this at length. As the concluding chapter argues, this tendency signals the possibility of a major distortion of the democratic process. If this tendency persists, the very basis of democratic India could be corroded. The critical question is whether India is absorbing the traits of majoritarianism or whether it is likely to withstand the majoritarian temptations.

Third, since the 2014 elections, the relationship between democracy and nationalism came under pressure. While the argument is proffered among some circles that nationalism is antithetical to democracy, a counterargument that seems to be gaining ground and apparently receiving public approbation is that a normative ordering between these two is required in favour of nationalism, and that nationalism is the richer, more valuable moral narrative compared to democracy. This juxtaposition of nationalism and democracy results into pushing people to choosing between the two. The subtext seems to be that more than democracy, nationalism has the power of moral superiority and also the potential of realizing the goal of 'development'. Indications are that people might be willing to tweak democracy for purposes of perceived ideas of nationalism and national interest. Will democracy then become the normative goal of the second order?

On the whole, the current moment suddenly makes democracy look like a fragile project. This book does not go into the specific details of these three critical issues, but it was shaped in the shadow of these issues, and it hopes to encourage the reader to relate to these contemporary challenges while making sense of the complex project called 'Democracy in India'.

Acknowledgements

Writing this 'short' introduction has meant I have incurred disproportionately large debts. In the process of presenting a summary of various complex issues, I have relied on the rich pre-existing scholarship on various aspects of democratic politics in India. While the bibliography would give some idea of this borrowing, the discernible reader would also notice the many unspecified borrowings on which this tract is based. I would therefore like to acknowledge the debt of colleagues from whom this tract learns a lot.

More specifically, I would like to acknowledge the following debts. One, I gratefully acknowledge the encouraging and insightful reviews of the initial proposal by two anonymous colleagues. Two, the manuscript has benefitted from the critical comments of two anonymous reviewers. Three, during the more than one decade of my academic and intellectual association with Yogendra Yadav, I have learnt a great deal—sharing many ideas and concerns about contemporary politics. If one finds some reflection of those ideas and concerns in this tract, it is certainly not a coincidence! Finally, Rajeshwari Deshpande spared time to read the early draft of the chapters and gave detailed feedback.

Parts of this tract were presented at the Moin Shakir Memorial Lectures at the political science department of Dr Babasaheb Ambedkar Marathwada University, Aurangabad, Maharashtra, India (in January 2017) and the Rajni Kothari Lecturer Series at Centre for Public Policy, Habitat and Human Development at Tata Institute of Social Sciences, Mumbai, India (in February 2017). These have given me the opportunity to present some of the ideas from this short introduction and receive feedback from the audiences.

At a personal level, I wish to acknowledge Rekha Palshikar for supporting not just this work, but my various other academic pretensions.

The editors at Oxford University Press consistently persuaded me to take up this work and patiently piloted it through the various steps of pre-publication preparations, and I am grateful to them.

Abbreviations

AD	Akali Dal
ADR	Association for Democratic Reforms
AFSPA	Armed Forces (Special Powers) Acts
AIADMK	All India Anna Dravida Munnetra Kazhagam
BJD	Biju Janata Dal
BJP	Bharatiya Janata Party
BKD	Bharatiya Kranti Dal
BKU	Bharatiya Kisan Union
BLD	Bharatiya Lok Dal
BSP	Bahujan Samaj Party
CAG	Comptroller and Auditor General
DMK	Dravida Munnetra Kazhagam
ECI	Election Commission of India
ENP	Effective Number of Parties
JD	Janata Dal

NDA	National Democratic Alliance
OBC	Other Backward Classes
RJD	Rashtriya Janata Dal
RPI	Republican Party of India
RSS	Rashtriya Swayamsevak Sangh
SC	Scheduled Caste
SEZ	Special Economic Zone
SP	Samajwadi Party
ST	Scheduled Tribe
TRS	Telangana Rashtra Samiti
ULFA	United Liberation Front of Assam
UPA	United Progressive Alliance

1

India's Democracy
Many Assessments

Democracy is professed more easily than it is prac-
tised. People approve of it as an ideal, but its practise
leaves much to be desired. The experience in India is
no exception. Widespread support for democracy has
characterized the life of democracy in India in the last
seven decades.

It is indeed true that India has had a longer history
of conversation in the language of democracy. In one
limited sense, this conversation had its starting point in
the 'national movement'—in demands for representation and self-rule (swaraj)—that emerged around the
beginning of the twentieth century. These early voices
of Naoroji and Tilak later culminated in demand for
complete independence and a demand for a constitution prepared by Indians themselves. But democracy

is not only about electing a government, nor is it only about freedom from a foreign power. The relations between the rulers and the ruled cannot become democratic unless there is openness about who can become the ruler and about how the rulers treat the ruled.

Moreover, democracy is fundamentally about all power relations—among members of society and among social groups. In this sense, India's encounter with democracy can be traced back to the nineteenth century itself. It was then that a deep churning began in Indian society—partly occasioned by the colonial encounter, but more substantively by the historic interface between tradition and modernity. This was the early stage of democratization of social relations (between men and women, among different sects, religions, and, most importantly, among castes), known as the beginning of 'social reform' and consequent democratization of the idea of power. This churning involved questions about the worth of women and men as individuals, and it also questioned the hierarchical social arrangements characterized by caste. In these debates and struggles, democratic logic was almost invariably employed. Thus, in the nineteenth century, Jyotirao Phule might not have specifically used the language of representative democracy; nevertheless, his attack on caste and his appeal to adopt equality as the cardinal value were certainly an integral part of the democratic conversation that was shaping in the nineteenth century. Phule's writings and activities are thus pioneering for modern democracy in India because he contested the prevailing ideas and arrangement of power and sought to mobilize public opinion. Thus, the two key features of India's democracy began to shape through the late nineteenth century—*contestations* over ideas and power sharing, and popular *mobilization* for the pursuit of those claims.

Both contestations and mobilizations often happened in clumsy and complicated manner. On the one hand, the project to construct a united national identity was undergoing, and it sought to reconcile aspirations of different sections, often privileging the 'national' over everything else. On the other, competing claims were emerging from, and on the basis of, caste, religion, and ethnicity. These not only competed with each other; they claimed primacy over the national claims, or, in the case of religion, claimed a counter-idea of nation itself. This was reflected more and more in the nationalist rhetoric of the twentieth century and in the negotiations with the colonial rulers. The competing claims even shaped separate political platforms that entered into the limited arena of electoral competition from the 1920s onwards. Both these, the shaping of the national (all-India and nationalist) claims as well as the rise of competing claims to occupy critical space in the national arena, constituted the backdrop in which democratic politics of independent India evolved.

The history of democratic politics during the colonial period resulted in the rise of three terrains of politics in the post-Independence era: politics around institutions; politics around formal governmental power (electoral politics); and politics around socio-political transformation (politics of movements). Needless to say, these three often overlapped and influenced each other.

Politics of institutions had already begun to shape during the colonial era—over questions of representation, the structure of the legislatures, the nature of the executive, and so on. That time, the debates were mainly in the threefold context of colonialism, Hindu–Muslim competition, and claims of different caste groups, mainly the oppressed castes. Drafting of the Constitution was a huge exercise in the politics over institutions, but making the Constitution did not conclude that politics; instead, the Constitution provided for a basis for that politics to continue later. Contestations emerged between the judiciary and the parliament over the meaning of constitutional provisions. The centre and states often disagreed over distribution of power. The legislatures and executives engaged in competition over the question of superiority. As the institutional practices matured, many other

4

institutions entered the arena of democratic contestations; these included the Election Commission of India
(ECI), which grew powerful and visible suddenly during the 1990s; or the Comptroller and Auditor General
(CAG) or the Information Commissioner's office, both
of which came into the limelight much later, after
2000. The bureaucracy, too, has always been a more or
less visible player in this power game. Thus, a continuous stream of claims and counterclaims constituted the
politics of institutions producing welcome restraints on
institutions, fearsome excesses, and worrisome inertia.
These contestations were played out in courts, in parliamentary proceedings, in corridors of bureaucratic
offices, and, increasingly, also in the media.

Immediately after the commencement of the
Constitution, India plunged itself into electoral politics
based on open competition and adult franchise, despite
doubts among international observers and sections of
Indian elite. Over time, the 'gamble' of holding open
and free party competition through nationwide elections has turned out so successful that it has almost
acquired mythical proportions. Since 1951, elections
have not only taken place with regularity (with the
exception of the Emergency), they have been an exciting and keenly contested affair. In the period prior
to the 1990s, electoral violence and malpractices did
occur on a large scale, but that has almost become a

matter of the past now. More importantly, despite these problems, electoral outcomes have ordinarily been received as legitimate and are routinely accepted by contesting parties. Defeated parties have only on rare occasions seriously challenged the outcomes of elections. There have always been a large number of parties contesting elections, but during the 1990s the number of parties represented in the Lok Sabha increased sizably. Simply put, the number of serious contenders in elections has increased and India has moved from a one-party dominance system to a multiparty system. This is more technically calculated by means of the effective number of parties (ENP), and ENP indicates the competitiveness and inclusiveness of the party system. By this token, the Lok Sabha became much more competitive and inclusive after 1989 because the ENP went up both in terms of votes and seats during this period. In terms of seats, the ENP was 1.4 in 1984; this went up to 5 and more than 5 in the post-1996 period. In the same period, the ENP, in terms of votes, went up to 7 from 4 in 1984. The number of parties represented in the Lok Sabha too has seen an increase: both in 2009 and 2014, as many as 36 parties were represented in Lok Sabha (Palshikar and Suri 2014: 40).

While the ruling party at the centre changed only in 1977 for the first time, since then, it has changed 7 times out of the 10 elections that took place. Party alternation became quite common in the states since 1967, and between 1989 and 2000, assembly elections were often seen as graveyards of sitting governments. So not only has there been an expansion in the number of contenders, there has also been an increase in the number of parties getting to share power either nationally or in some state. This numeric expansion notwithstanding, the electoral arena has thrown up critical questions about the space for serious policy differences. Whether the electoral arena effectively produces competition of ideas and policies or leads to a convergence among the players, thus producing closure of substantive competition, is a key question about the electoral arena. It is precisely this limitation of the electoral arena that makes the terrain of movements more attractive for those who want democratic politics to make a difference to policies, procedures, and outcomes.

Contestations over ideas, issues, and power never remained confined only to electoral competition. Democracy always came to be understood as the right of people and groups to mobilize outside the electoral arena and to bring pressure both on governments and parties. Thus, the terrain of mass movements has always been vibrant and integral to democratic contestations. There is hardly any issue or agenda that has not generated collective mobilization outside the routine sphere of party politics. In fact, collective mobilizations have always facilitated the expression of many interests and issues that the arena of party politics might be less willing to take up. The terrain of movements has thus straddled the universes of cross-party issues of concerns as also issues not much amenable to the electoral considerations of parties. Besides the communist-led movements of peasants, movements for linguistic states occupied this terrain in the immediate post-Independence period. Trade unions, too, had a large existence right from those early days. Since the late 1970s, the farmers' movements initiated by middle farmers became voluble, but at the same time movements for women's rights, environmental issues, civil rights, Adivasis' rights to access to the forests, and many other new movements also came to the forefront. These were at one point described as 'new' social movements. Even during the time when movements were seen to be weak (post 1980s), politics always witnessed small groups challenging the policies and ideas of the ruling elite. The Narmada Bachao Andolan was probably the most influential among such movements. All these movements, through large scale mobilizations as also more specific issue-based mobilizations, made it possible for citizens to participate in the political process and intervene in the debates about power sharing and policy formulations. Electoral arena facilitates this in a more restricted and formal manner through campaigns and voting. Movements facilitate such participation more directly and in a substantive manner. That is why mobilizations around broader issues and agenda are important in shaping the democratic process. However, the disjunction between parties and movements and the inability of movements to sustain the momentum have been key issues pertaining to the movement terrain.

This short introduction possibly cannot go into the detailed history of India's democratic politics, nor can it undertake an elaborate critical analysis of India's democracy. For that purpose, a rich body of literature is available. (For details, see the Bibliography at the end of the book.) The primary objective of this tract is to initiate an informed debate, not only among the experts, but also among the larger reading public, over many critical issues surrounding India's democracy leading to informed assessments.

Evaluations of democracy are always likely to be trapped between romanticism and cynicism. Romanticism would publicize the success of democracy, while cynicism would pessimistically pronounce the (many) failures of democracy. In particular, discussions in the public forums and in media often get entangled in this dichotomy of success and failure. Academic literature, on the other hand, is often immersed in comparisons. So, success or failure would be seen mainly in comparison to other democracies. Though valuable, such comparisons tend to lose the temporal and context-specific richness of insights. Internationally, there has been considerable interest among scholars on the issue of democracy's performance. In such analyses, it is quite customary to resort to the language of recession or deficit. Assessments are based on the extent of demand for democracy by citizens and the supply of democracy by elites and institutions. Most assessments end up resorting to 'ranking'. Most 'rankings' are open to two criticisms. One, they adopt a culturally biased Western model of democracy as the standard, and, two, they rely much too heavily on either external or elite evaluations. The various exercises of comparing democracy's performance through rankings place India in the middling group—much below the many European democracies and, interestingly, even below many non-Western democracies that appear to be strictly following the West in terms of institutional arrangements (Mongolia!). The central concern of all such rankings is the institutional weaknesses and less-than-adequate prevalence of the liberal democratic norm of civil rights. See, for instance, the website of World Democracy Audit, which ranks Mongolia at 36 and India at 48 (World Democracy Audit 2001), or the Freedom House website that gives India a score of 77 out of 100 (Freedom House 2017).

Since the early twentieth century, more and more societies have been attracted to democracy, making democracy the most accepted goal in all parts of the globe. This geographic expansion of democracy is often matched by the lament about its lack of depth. Everyone loves to proclaim commitment to democracy, and yet the continuity, maturity, and stability of democratic practices are found to be shaky. Hence, the language of deficits and recessions. Of course, even the so-called older democracies, too, face ups and downs, undergo recessions, and experience deficit. Evaluation of India's democracy is no exception to this broader pattern. Internationally, India's democracy is simultaneously a subject of awe because of its scale and dogged continuity over seven decades, and also subject of some scepticism because of its many drawbacks particularly in procedural realm, where it does not necessarily fit the standards set by North Atlantic experiences.

Domestically, India's democracy is quite vibrant in terms of the diversity of its critical evaluations. Here, too, the self-congratulatory pronouncements of success of the world's largest democracy notwithstanding, there are severe indictments of India's democracy on four grounds. One, it is argued that there is nothing 'Indian' about it and that we have been aping the Western model of democracy without much respect for indigenous democratic traditions. This criticism, mostly emanating from the Hindu nationalist perspective, was more vocal at the time of the making of the Constitution and immediately thereafter. Though muted, it still occupies space in the minds of many of the Hindutva supporters and is used conveniently by some hardliners from time to time. Two, it is argued that the democracy we have adopted does not in reality leave any room for people to decide their fate—again, this criticism, too, would fault it for its blind adoption of the Western model and argue that a true democracy should posit all power with the people at the grassroots—a mixture of direct democracy and local democracy is wistfully contrasted to our 'representative' democracy. It may be recalled here that in the course of the anti-corruption agitation of 2011, its key leaders Anna Hazare and Arvind Kejriwal often resonated this sentiment. Ostensibly, this line of thinking has its roots in the Gandhian way of looking at participatory and local democracy. Three, critics argue that India's present democracy is nothing but a sham because it perpetrates the power and privileges of the established, dominant interests, the landlords, and the capitalists. This sham is contrasted to real—people's—democracy by this genre of criticism. Such criticisms can be broadly identified with the Marxist way of thinking. This form of criticism has been quite influential in academic circles in India. Though identified with Marxism, soon

12

after Independence the Communist Party nuanced this criticism and subsequently toned it down. Later, the Maoists came to be identified with such a drastic rejection of existing democracy. They continue to do so, both intellectually and through action, even today. Four, India's democracy is faulted for not following the democratic principles as they have evolved in the West. Mainly coming from those who believe in the importance of rules and procedures and the sanctity of institutions, this criticism resonates the concerns and criticisms of the liberal democratic analyses. According to this criticism, India has not adequately succeeded in ensuring robust liberal traditions of individual dignity and freedom.

In more recent times, a somewhat different line of criticism is developing. It argues that India's democracy is becoming mostly or only 'electoral' democracy. This implies that there is excessive emphasis on elections and nothing beyond; it also implies that while elections are indeed democratic, in the spheres beyond elections—in social relations and non-electoral political practice—there is much to be desired. Perhaps, a more robust criticism would be that India's democracy has failed in its own criteria of performance. Take, for instance, the dispersal of power to all people, or inclusion of all sections in the scheme of power, or the welfare of the entire society, or the challenge of wiping every tear from every eye—none of these objectives are adequately fulfilled or, for that matter, not even pursued seriously through the many contestations that democracy has opened up.

In contrast to somewhat harsh and negative assessments by scholars, experts, and the activists, people themselves seem to have a somewhat indulgent view of how democracy functions in India. Overall, people are 'satisfied' with the way in which democracy functions—this is the finding of two nationally representative surveys spread across almost a decade. (Data collected as part of the South Asia–wide survey to study people's assessment of democracy—SDSA Team 2008; Lokniti 2015.) And yet, there are many inconsistencies and ambiguities that mark India's democracy. So, assessments of democracy cannot be merely in the form of complacent approval just as they need not be pronouncements of failure.

In the chapters that follow, the moments of democratic achievements, the areas of concern, and the many spaces of ambiguity that mark the march of democracy in India are discussed.

2

The Institutional Context
How Democratic Is It?

Institutions have a complex and double-edged relationship with democracy. They formalize and protect democracy; they also circumscribe democracy by creating entrenched structures of formal power. One cannot only despise the institutional paraphernalia just as one cannot rest assured by its existence. The relationship of institutions and democracy in India is no different. This peculiar relationship means that actual outcomes would depend more on the performance of institutions than mere debates over design. The Constitution of India has always remained the fountain of authority to ensure democracy. It has almost become the anthem of democracy in India and inspired democratic institution making in many new democracies.

It has received scholarly approval from many quarters and, so far, it has stood the severe test of time in the seven decades of its existence. Nevertheless, the functioning of various institutions has always given rise to dissatisfaction among citizens and downright anxieties among scholars. It is this irony of the coexistence of carefully thought-out constitutional document and a much-to-be-desired institutional practice that constitutes a critical disjunction on which democracy in India is predicated.

This chapter draws attention to this disjunction and the inconsistencies in performance of institutions as also the precariousness of the institutional ability to protect and advance democracy. In a sense, this ambivalent nature of relationship of institutions with democracy is in tune with the larger point this book makes: that democracy in India is a somewhat inconsistent enterprise full of paradoxes and contradictory possibilities.

Though many institutions have been created subsequent to the making of the Constitution, the larger institutional architecture draws its logic and legitimacy from the Constitution itself. The Constitution is a document that is alive to the tension between order and democracy, between state intervention and freedom, between autonomy of state institutions and the possibility of their takeover by entrenched interests. Therefore, the Constitution seeks to do three things. One, whenever possible, it strikes a balance—a golden mean—on matters of both theory and practice of state power. Two, it creates a web of checks and counter-checks to ensure institutional balance. And three, it allows the unfolding of competitive claims over the state by different societal interests through a demo-cratic contestation. What emerges is a 'weak-strong' state that vacillates between welfare and neglect, between facilitating democratic spaces and exercis-ing repressive energy. The Constitution expects the state and its institutional machinery to function autonomously from entrenched interests and become an instrument of social transformation in a selective manner. This would allow the state to become a site of contestations among competing claims. In reality, the state emerges as a web of institutions that often fail to satisfy citizens and end up being instruments of dominance rather than instruments of advancing democracy. This is not due to the Constitution, but is more a result of the functioning of institutions and the multiple inabilities to balance institutions with popular assertions. Thus, the universe of India's institutions of governance is marked by the inconsistency between purpose and performance.

Maai–Baap without Trust

Perhaps the most explicit case of such inconsistency is the popular perception of institutions. From Independence onwards, the Indian state has initiated innumerable policies, schemes, and programmes for the 'welfare' of the population in general and of the weaker sections in particular. Governments have vied with each other and party manifestoes compete with each other in listing or promising new schemes and allocating large budgetary provisions for this. A huge development bureaucracy emanated from these initiatives. The extent to which this is done has prompted critics to ridicule the transformation of the state institutions into maai–baap—parents of citizens; this has also prompted scholars to describe India's democratic politics as patronage democracy and the Indian state as paternal state authority. Critics of the welfare regime have always complained that overactive state has created a dependent citizenry lacking in initiative. Given this overemphasis on the state's welfare role, one would expect that the speed of attaining the well-being of citizens would be rapid and also that citizens would be deeply enamoured of the state and its institutions.

On both counts, the reality is contrary. Poverty alleviation has been slow; overall performance on Human Development Indicators has been unsatisfactory; health care, quality education, and so on, remain distant dreams; indebtedness is the single most critical factor ailing agriculture; unemployment in both rural and urban areas is alarming. (As per United Nations Development Programme's *Human Development Reports*, on a scale of 0 to 1, India's Human Development Index has marginally moved from 0.4 in 1990 to 0.6 in 2015; ranking 131 among 188 countries [*Human Development Report* 2016].) So, the welfare state as an institution envisioned by the Constitution did not come about despite a huge institutional network created by successive governments. These institutions are ensconced in authority, but the outcome has been somewhat lacklustre.

Secondly, and not surprisingly, popular trust in many institutions is only moderate. The analogy of maai–baap does not reflect the popular perceptions of the institutions. Data from two surveys spread across a decade (2004–5 and 2013) reveals that most institutions suffer from low trust levels. Very few people have high (great deal of) trust in most institutions. Moreover, if we take into account negative assessment (where respondents say they do not have much trust or have no trust at all), then the 'net' trust is often negative in case of many institutions. Barely one in every five persons has robust level (great deal) of trust in bureaucracy at both these points in time (20 and 18 per cent in 2013 and 2005, respectively); while the police were trusted by even a lesser proportion of surveyed respondents (16 and 17 per cent). For both civil servants and police, negative assessment (those who did not have much trust or did not trust at all) outnumbered those who had a great deal of trust—the net score for civil service was −19 and −6, and for police −27 and −29, respectively. In contrast, the armed forces and courts enjoy greater trust. Army happens to be the most highly trusted institution (57 and 51 per cent in 2013 and 2005, respectively). Political parties are the least trusted institution—with 10 and 13 per cent having robust trust and the net trust pegged at −13 in 2013 and −9 in 2005. More specifically, in 2013, only 19 per cent persons fully agreed that the government would do the right things to solve people's problems, with 14 per cent completely disagreeing with this suggestion. Not surprisingly, only 6 per cent believe that the government will solve the problem they think is the most urgent one (Lokniti 2015; SDSA Team 2008).

The relatively greater trust enjoyed by the army, courts, or ECI, in contrast to parties and government, should alarm any supporter of democracy for two reasons. One, they are non-elected institutions in contrast to the elected or popular institutions with low trust levels. Two, it suggests a possibility that institutions gain trust when they are distant from regular contact, while people have less trust when they come in to more frequent contact with various institutions. But it is precisely these institutions—parties and government—that one would expect to ensure and enrich democracy. Weak trust in them would mean that popular confidence in democracy would erode in the long run if these institutions do not improve their functioning.

More worryingly, institutions and their operation are often perceived as mired in corruption. Thus, if we understand public confidence as a key test of the democratic nature of public institutions, most would fail the test.

Landmark Failures

Democracy hinges on regulation of power while institutions enjoy the power of regulation. This paradox is sought to be resolved by creating 'democratic conditions' for the functioning of institutions through complex and delicate internal balance based on the principle of checks and balances. To begin with, each institution has to operate within a frame of self-regulation (self-restraint); second, institutions need to be amenable to mutual control or regulation ('checks and balances'); and third, institutions should be open to popular control (accountability and responsiveness). The institutional architecture provided by the

Constitution indeed contains these three elements. The actual functioning of institutions, however, does not approximate that architecture many times.

There have been some rather worrying and dramatic instances that can be described as 'landmark failures' of institutional practice. Three of them pertain to intercommunity relations and the responsibility of state institutions to ensure both 'law and order' and more substantively protect the foundational principle of diversity. These instances include the anti-Sikh riots of 1984, mob vandalism of the mosque at Ayodhya in 1992, and large-scale massacre of Muslims in Gujarat in 2002. In all three, complicity of the police and political establishments was alleged. In all three, no justice has come about in terms of systematic imposition of penalties on perpetrators. In all three, political forces involved in the violation of the democratic norm have gone scot free—legally as well as politically. Thus, more than the fact of such occurrences having taken place, the institutional inability to ensure effective and timely punishment marks the failure. They deserve to be chronicled as landmark failures because of the multiple failures involved—failure of principles, failure of constitutional morality, failure of spirit of democracy, and failure of various institutions of governance.

The entire episode revolving around the imposition of Emergency in 1975 exemplifies in a most instructive manner this malady of living with landmark failures. While it can be argued that the original provision for declaring emergency on grounds of internal distur-bance (subsequently amended) was loose enough for unscrupulous political actors taking undue advantage, the declaration and implementation of that Emergency in 1975 also chronicles failure of the three 'control' mechanisms mentioned earlier. Following a historic mandate and the credit for having defeated Pakistan military in the Bangladesh War of 1971, the Congress government led by Indira Gandhi faced popular unrests—initially in Gujarat and Bihar, but later across many parts of the country. The growing unity among the opposition parties, the railway strike, and veteran leader Jayaprakash Narayan's appeal to police and security forces not to obey 'illegal' orders, all cre-ated an atmosphere of uncertainty. The decision of the Allahabad High Court invalidating Indira Gandhi's Lok Sabha election of 1971 added to the tensions. This was also the moment when Indira Gandhi was reportedly relying more and more on a small group of advisors rather than consulting her party colleagues or cabinet colleagues. The dramatic rise of her son Sanjay Gandhi was another extraordinary feature of this moment. The clash between the government and the judiciary added to the political tensions of the period. These events between 1973 and 1975 led Indira Gandhi to argue that a situation of anarchy was being created deliberately and that there was an international conspiracy to destabilize India. Therefore, she—without consulting the cabinet—asked the president to declare a state of emergency under Article 352 of the Constitution on the ground that there was an internal threat to the country's security and law and order. This led to the imprisonment of political opponents, excessive use of preventive detentions, and suspension of fundamental rights altogether. This episode needs to be remembered as representing multiple failures of institutions of democracy.

The executive displayed utter disregard to the spirit of the constitution and failed in self-regulation. This failure involved the law ministry, attorney general, prime minister's office, the top leadership of ruling party, the president, senior ministers, and senior bureaucrats. That failure of self-regulation was compounded by the inability of the Parliament and judiciary to regulate the excesses of the executive—the principle of 'checks and balances' thus became completely infructuous in that instance. The third resort, that is, public regulation, also did not work because the press was gagged and could not (rather did not) fight out the issue of censorship—leaders of opposition parties were arrested, their cadres were clueless about how to continue public protests in the light of repression, and general public was not so incensed as to take to streets even when basic freedoms were suspended. Only the coincidence of many circumstances finally brought about in 1977 an electoral defeat of the party and government imposing emergency. That 'happy ending' depended upon Indira Gandhi's decision to hold elections, the unity of the opposition parties, the long-standing rot within the Congress party, and the media intervention that sought to retaliate retrospectively. But so long as the emergency was in place, there was no strong popular resistance vis-à-vis either the bureaucracy or the political rulers.

While the Emergency and what happened during it indeed indicated political failure, it was also an institutional failure—to ensure counterchecks and ensure protection of democracy. Instead of protecting democracy, the institutional edifice became complicit in endangering democracy during 1975–7. Of course, it could be argued that the Emergency was an extreme instance. But it alerts us to the complete collapse of accountability, a cynical abdication of bureaucratic responsibility, and narrow use of judicial authority as well. So, it was not merely a case of political actors going wrong and misusing the mandate; the bureaucracy too became a willing tool in the suspension of democratic process and the judiciary failed to rise to the occasion since it chose to interpret its power in a restrictive manner. Hence, the Emergency became a monument of institutional failure in adhering to and protecting democracy.

Question of Institutional Equilibrium

Besides such major failures, institutional life in India is also faced with the issue of institutional balance of powers. Democracies require balanced relations among its institutions. Constitutions often outline such balance of powers, so that no institution can overwhelm others, but, at the same time, institutional deadlock too does not take place. This issue partly concerns the executive and judiciary, but, besides that, in routine practice all institutions of governance need to be circumscribed by the ethic of equilibrium.

The adoption of the parliamentary form modelled on the British pattern gave rise to an expectation that the Parliament would be the supreme institution—as protector of democracy. But often the Parliament has ceded ground to the executive and its urge to restrict freedoms in favour of national security and law and order. This has been witnessed right from the first amendment restricting right to speech to various more or less draconian legislations including the preventive detention legislations, anti-terror legislations, and the most debated Armed Forces (Special Powers) Acts

(AFSPA), giving the armed forces special powers in 'disturbed areas'. This has resulted into allowing the Indian state to become more and more a regulating agency alone—obsessed with issues of 'law and order', giving more and more powers to the police and military apparatuses and going to the extent of justifying unregulated 'encounters'. Instead of strengthening the British tradition of legislative oversight and protection of citizen rights, institutional practice has imitated the colonial legacy of using repressive measures without adequate safeguards. While the 'special powers' of the armed forces have always been a contentious issue in both North East and Jammu and Kashmir, the core point is how the Indian state perceives itself. The answer is that the Indian state perceives itself as the legatee of the colonial tendency of suspicion and highhandedness rather than an agent of the Indian Constitution.

Besides working in collaboration with the executive on the issue of law and order, the Parliament also easily ceded overall initiative to the executive. Though it lost its real powers to the executive pretty early in the course of post-Independence developments, the real battle occurred on the issue of interpreting the Constitution and amending it. This was seen as the debate over parliamentary sovereignty, but in reality the issue turned out to be the turf war between the executive and the judiciary. After considerable ups and downs, the issue of relationship between the Parliament and judiciary was settled by the Supreme Court ruling of 1973 in the Kesavananda Bharti Case. While giving latitude to the Parliament in deciding policies, the court reserved to itself the responsibility of deciding and protecting the basic features of the Constitution. But in the post-1973 period, the exercise of judicial power often stretched the principle of basic features. This has happened through two routes. One, in the matter of appointments to high courts and the Supreme Court, the judiciary has practically excluded the executive, and attempts to modify this arrangement have been nullified. This has made India's judiciary almost self-appointed. While this adds to the power, prestige, and autonomy of the judiciary, it tends to upset the delicate balance between judiciary and 'government'. Two, from the 1980s, the courts have resorted to consistent broadening of the scope of judicial interventions inviting the criticism of judicial 'overreach' or judicial activism. The practice of 'public interest litigation' received support from many civil society groups working for marginalized sections. But whether judicial interventions should settle political questions is a debatable matter.

While this overreach has sometimes resulted into better protection of rights, more positive interpretations of the rights provisions, and even democratization in terms of greater space for public scrutiny and vigilance of political actors, it still begs the fundamental question: should a democratic system hinge on institutional imbalance and frequent intervention by the judiciary?

Those who defend active judiciary would point out that in many instances of such alleged judicial overreach, two issues are invariably entangled. One is the issue of legislative and/or executive abdication of responsibilities. It is argued that judiciary steps in when legislature or executive fail to apply their powers for the furtherance of public interest. In the period since the 1980s, the judiciary mandated many policy initiatives chiefly because the 'governments' shrank away from responsibilities. In a sense, then, the overreach was matching the underperformance of key institutions of governance. So, the real crisis was not about judicial overreach, but the inability of governments to adequately address issues of governance. Two, many instances of 'overreach' also relate to the inability of competitive politics to regulate itself. Parties and legislatures have often been less than willing to ensure democratic regulation of competition. Hence, the question of electoral reform has always been consigned to the backburner. Since 'politics' fails to reform itself, the judiciary steps in to enforce some mechanisms of regulation.

Thus, the issue is much wider in its scope than merely judicial overreach. It is about elected/popular institutions failing in their duty to self-regulate and, therefore, non-elected institutions stepping in to 'make politics democratic'. This same argument was invoked when, during the 1990s, the ECI chose to handle electoral malpractices with a heavy hand and practically treated political parties as the accused. Much of the popularity of the ECI stems from its overreach. Judiciary, ECI, and many other important institutions created by the Constitution or by statute are necessary components of democratic functioning. While they draw their authority from the Constitution, the Constitution also upholds the basic principle of democracy, that is, people are the source of authority, and representatives are the instruments of expressing that authority. We are thus faced with the clash between 'elected' popular authority and 'constitutional' authority.

More importantly, the justifications of overreach (underperformance and/or political failure) still beg a larger question: if institutions do not perform or if institutions shirk the responsibility to self-regulate, why is it that there is no public reprisals of these failures? Civil society organizations working for better governance and for electoral reform have to take recourse to a judicial route instead of the democratic route of popular mobilization on these issues. Thus, while the judiciary or ECI can be faulted for stepping in into what is essentially a matter of public intervention, the real shortcoming is that there is not enough assurance that public mobilization can indeed take place or political actors would be deterred from transgressions for fear of public reaction. In the wake of failure of the political route, a non-political route is chosen for correcting politics. Hence, the real problem is not of judicial overreach, but of external (and non-political) correction of the course of institutional performance. This problem exacerbates the institutional imbalance.

Half-hearted Democracy

India is often described as the 'largest' democracy because of the size of its electorate. Even in terms of reasonably good record of enrolment of citizens in voters' list and the consistent and globally comparable turnout nearing or crossing 60 per cent in parliamentary elections, India would qualify as a very large and successful electoral democracy (the highest turnout so far was recorded in 2014 at 66.4 per cent). The regularity of elections (barring the postponement in 1976) is another feature symbolizing the successful institutionalization of the system of elections. The feat of holding elections almost peacefully and on a regular basis is certainly no mean achievement.

But precisely because of the size and scale, it becomes more than necessary that India should have multiple mechanisms to ensure greater transparency in the government's functioning, that there should be more opportunities for citizens to hold office bearers more accountable, and there should be more avenues for citizen participation in politics. But institutions are often unwilling to incorporate such mechanisms. Performance of institutions would mostly fall short on the principles of transparency, accountability, and participation. While structural arrangements can be faulted only partially for this shortfall, the real 'deficit' arises from practice. Formal machineries for these purposes could not be easily installed because parties and governments have always hesitated in expanding the scope of democracy. And when new mechanisms are put in place, their functioning often remains restrictive rather than inclusive.

Governments are often shrouded in mystery protected by secrecy. This secrecy percolates to all government functionaries and offices resulting in harassment of the citizen and hiding of corrupt practices. The long battle for right to information by many activists and organizations finally brought about the Right to Information Act (2005). However, instead of altering the ways in which institutions function, it has ended up in creating a new bureaucracy—the machinery to monitor the implementation of the right to information. Governments and institutions have yet not evolved the culture of transparency. This is evident from the unwillingness to part with information voluntarily. Thus, the Act is in place, but its spirit—transparent governance—is missing. Similarly, the struggle for accountability has had only limited success in the real sense. Representatives are not accountable to voters on a regular basis except when seeking re-election. No clear procedures are in place to avoid conflict of interest—both for the bureaucracy and for the political representatives. The struggle for establishing people's ombudsman (Lokpal and Lokayukt) is too famous even to require a mention. A demand dating back to late1960s was finally met only in 2013. The Lokpal Bill was passed only after a dramatic struggle staged in New Delhi during 2011–12. Even then, accountability is still a distant dream, and the ombudsman machinery is either invisible or ineffective. Not many states have effective Lokayukt machinery. For more than three years since the Lokpal Act was passed, appointment of Lokpal dragged on. So, here, too, only half-hearted steps are taken to placate popular protests—without necessarily making substantive institutional reform. People's participation has met with similar fate. Parties are enthusiastic in running membership drives, but slow or unresponsive to demands for intra-party democracy. The 73rd and 74th Constitutional Amendments introduced citizen participation in local institutions of government through gram sabha and ward/area sabha mechanisms. However, these mechanisms are not even nominally followed. Thus, democratic principles are adopted formally and followed in rather opaque and indirect mechanisms, but when citizens demand more direct involvement with routine functioning of institutions, such demands are avoided or sabotaged.

Institutional Failure?

Is then democracy through institutions a failed project?

Institutions have failed to maintain a dignified balance; they have failed to employ their powers for public good; they have failed to accommodate the democratic impulse of citizens; they even fail to recognize people as rightful citizens. The culture of institutions is imbued with suspicion of 'people' or is happy to treat citizens as customers or beneficiaries only. It is also true that institutional practices give rise to the dichotomy between institutions and the people. Institutions often turn into fortresses of power from which citizens are excluded and which operate directly against rights and dignity of the citizens. India's democratic talent has failed to ensure that institutions would genuinely perform in a pro-people manner.

Democracy through institutions requires the prevalence of the liberal democratic ethic based on 'rule of law'. The Constitution indeed vigorously invokes this principle. However, the history of the evolution of the idea and practice of democracy in India has not adequately sought to bring this principle to the centre stage. Two factors have intervened in the path of rule of law. One is the emphasis on mobilization more than institutions during the colonial rule. Foreign rule meant more focus on mobilization and protests and less on working of institutions. The postcolonial democratic practice has not found it easy to balance this tradition of mobilization with the new requirement of institutional norms and practices. Two, social inequalities based on caste and community have produced a suspicion of institutions because of their tendency to be dominated by upper castes and majority community. Social reality made it difficult to balance equal rights of equal individuals with differential claims of castes and communities.

In spite of these shortcomings, the Constitution has indeed acquired the status of a haloed institution, and most of the social and political conflicts are often sought to be resolved within that framework. Similarly, the judiciary is seen as the custodian of rights and also seen as non-partisan. Then, the manner in which the prestige of the ECI has been built is noteworthy.

During the 1990s, the ECI shot to prominence because of its apparently anti-political stance, but the real source of its prestige is the smooth conduct of elections, the ability to reduce violence and malpractices, and, in more recent years, the constant drives to ensure greater inclusion of citizens through rigorous voter registration efforts. So, there are indications that institutionalization is slowly taking shape.

Another reason why the project need not be seen as a failure is the great social churning taking place in India's institutional arena both through the Constitution and through pressures of democratic politics. This churning relates to inclusiveness of institutions. The basis for the 'social engineering' happening in India is the Constitution itself. Through the provisions in Constitution, the scheduled castes (SCs) and scheduled tribes (STs) have been guaranteed representation in proportion to their share in population in both bureaucracy and legislatures. The social composition of many legislatures has transformed and others are following suit. (Jaffrelot and Sanjay Kumar 2009 enlist the details of this.) With this transformation, and the rise of a political elite from backward communities, and often from humble social backgrounds, the sociology of India's political elite has undergone a change. Following the 73rd and 74th Amendments strengthening the local bodies, not only members, but also office bearers of these bodies come from diverse backgrounds because of the provision of reservations for SCs, STs, Other Backward Classes (OBC), and women. This institutional device has brought into local power circles thousands of political actors from relatively marginalized backgrounds. Thus, while institutions fail to democratically respond to citizens, they have begun to be at least inclusive in a democratic manner. It would not be an exaggeration to say that contemporary administrative machinery and political office holders in India have shrugged off the imprint of upper-caste dominance at least in numerical terms.

If promise, performance, and personality are the three elements of institutional reality, India's institutional reality can boast of being high on promise; it can draw satisfaction from the gradual change of personality as well. Whether it would pass the critical test of performance is the key area of concern.

3

Regional Mobilizations

Different bases of public contestations emerge in a democratic society and take the form of political competition. Region is one among them. When different regions coexist within the framework of a common political arrangement, they tend to contest the prevailing balance of power vis-à-vis the larger political arrangements and also compete with each other on the question of resources and symbolic status of each region.

We often talk of 'Indian' politics. But Indian politics or Indian democracy is nothing if we do not take into consideration what happens in its many regions. This chapter gives an overview of the different expressions that regional politics assumes at different points in time and through which democratic mobilizations take place.

Three different claims have been made from time to time, and in different parts of the country, on the basis of region. One, and almost routinely, claims to statehood (and related matters such as greater share of central assistance or interstate disputes) have emerged within the institutional mechanism of federalism. Two, within many states, the issue of backwardness and 'regional imbalance' has become politically delicate where parts of the state have demanded various measures to ensure their fair share in development and power. Finally, claims have been made that a particular region is so different socially, historically, or emotionally that it deserves a separate political existence outside the Indian national framework—that people of that region aspire for an independent political existence.

Politics of Statehood

India's freedom movement produced a complex relationship between all-India or national loyalty and people's loyalties to their region. It is a cliché to say that nation comes first and the region comes only next. In reality, during the national movement, when people from a particular region would take up the national cause, their immediate point of reference would often be their own region, its history, and their local experience of colonial domination. Thus, the outbursts of nationalism in Bengal had a natural relationship to Bengali history and icons, expressions of nationalism in Marathi-speaking regions had an inevitable reference to Shivaji Maharaj, and nationalism in Rajasthan would predictably invoke the great battles fought by Maharana Pratap. These region-specific symbols continue to attract people of the respective regions even today. The national movement grew out of these region-based sentiments of national pride and, in the process, converted the regional symbols and sentiments into constitutive elements of nationalist claims for independence.

In other words, in order to understand and relate to the idea of nationhood, each region went back to its own history of self-assertion and glory—these were the regional gateways to the ongoing movement for national freedom. On the other hand, in due course, regional glory and identity were subsumed under national identity. Each region's pride and identity became integral to pride in Indian nationhood and national identity. Thus, the freedom movement unleashed regional assertions and, at the same time, tamed those assertions making them secondary to the overarching national or all-India claims.

This complex dynamics replayed itself in the post-Independence period also. The ideas of national unity and national development came to dominate. Yet 'region' emerged as an important theme around which much politics continued to occur. Just as India's new democratic politics was taking shape in the 1950s, people began to be conscious of the immediate reference point—politics around them, leaders around them, issues they could immediately relate to, language they could understand, and idiom of demands and claims that they could easily comprehend and be agitated about. To begin with, a new phase of reconstruction of regions became inevitable immediately after Independence. Many linguistic groups began demanding that regions with a common language should constitute political units of the new nation—the states. Continuing the practice to rediscover regional history and pride, their arguments often drew justification from historical memories, but in addition, now, the democratic argument, too, was marshalled. It was argued that popular demands needed a positive response from the system and that organizing politico-administrative units along language and popular wishes was only to be expected in a democratic setup. This gave rise to the movements for linguistic states mainly in the south and west of the country.

But the demand for linguistic states met with resistance from national leadership thus opening up the possibility of contest between national and regional elite. Nehru and Patel, along with other prominent members of the Indian government, felt that organizing the country administratively and politically on the basis of language and regional sentiments would hurt the delicate fabric of national unity in the backdrop of Partition. But leaders in the regions were strongly in favour of the demand and, in most cases, they did not budge even though towering leaders at the all-India level opposed the demand. In response to persistent demands, in 1956, the government of India had to undertake a major reorganization of states, though popular demands in today's Maharashtra and Gujarat, on the one hand, and Punjab and Haryana, on the other, were not satisfied that time. Maharashtra and Gujarat were created in 1960, and the 'linguistic' phase of creating states continued till 1966, when Punjab was reorganized on linguistic lines, and separate states of Punjab and Haryana were created.

Two decades of post-Independence period thus witnessed sustained popular mobilizations on the question of language-based states in the backdrop of considerable opposition from national leadership. During the agitations for linguistic states, the state-level leadership of the Congress party became strong vis-à-vis national leadership, and, in some instances, as in case of Punjab, these agitations strengthened the regional-level parties that were taking the lead for formation of separate state. This development is noteworthy for two reasons. One,

42

it indicates that local aspirations and demands could not be sidestepped easily—even at that early stage of post-Independence democratic politics, national leadership could not steamroll popular sentiment nor could it override local leadership. From Andhra to Maharashtra and Punjab, the local-level regional aspirations asserted notwithstanding the opposition of the all-India leadership. In both Maharashtra and Punjab, the agitation for forming language-based separate state sustained for a long duration. In fact, these agitations led to new ideas, search for historical justifications, rediscovery of linguistic pride, attempts to enrich literary tradition from respective languages, and the tryst to bring about well-being of the linguistic communities in consonance with the democratic spirit that was gaining ground. Hence, popular wishes and demands, expressed through sustained campaigns, overpowered national leadership. While Nehru continued to be the most popular leader, it did not deter the people from insisting on their demand for new states. The lesson was obvious: a leader, however popular, could not take the people for granted, and policies needed to be shaped in accordance with people's expectations.

Two, these movements threw up new leadership in each region. Both within the Congress party, which was ruling most of the regions in early post-Independence India, and within many non-Congress parties, language-based regional movements gave rise to new leaders who represented regional interests. The demands for statehood often pitted these new leaders against the national-level leadership of the Congress party. In a sense, this development symbolized the inevitable democratic dynamics of the emergence of the local elite competing with the national elite entrenched through their role in the national movement. In fact, it is possible to understand the politics of formation of new states as the process whereby local or regional political elite emerged and gained popular strength. This was a new and post-Independence generation of political elite (that is, the elite that emerged in the post-Independence era) which was to occupy central position in the politics of many states later.

Even after the first wave of forming new states—mostly on the basis of common language—demands for statehood resurfaced in different parts of the country and they have often been catalysts for new political forces in respective regions. While the period between 1970 and 1990 was marked by formation of smaller states mostly in the North East, from 2000 onwards, the new trend of division of existing large states had set in. Jharkhand had a long history of the demand for statehood, but such demands were somewhat muted or non-existent in Uttarakhand and Chhattisgarh.

The example of Telangana is instructive for the complications involved in regional demands, and the relationship between regional politics and regional demands. In fact, agitation by the Telugu-speaking part of the Madras province of post-Independence period was the first after Independence to demand statehood. The state of Andhra Pradesh was thus created setting aside the somewhat mute demand for a separate Telangana. The emotive issue of common language bypassed subregional dynamics only to surface again in the late 1960s when the agitation for a separate state of Telangana gathered momentum. Indira Gandhi managed to subdue that agitation, but it resurfaced after 2000 in the politically more volatile times with the rise of Telangana Rashtra Samiti (TRS). In the phase when Congress became weak nationally and also in the state, this agitation became even stronger, thus finally succeeding in the creation of the separate state of Telangana in 2014.

The politics of centre–state relations can also be viewed as an extension of politics of statehood. India's federal mechanism leaves much space for the centre to dominate in its relation with the states. This domination originates mainly in the powers of the centre to allocate resources to states in the form of grants besides the central mechanism of planning. But besides the issue of grants, appointment of governors, role of the governor, and imposition of president's rule, are notoriously famous irritants in centre–state relations. In particular, controversies surrounding centre–state relations often take the shape of competition among parties when different parties are in power at the centre and the state. For instance, Akali Dal (AD) and Dravida Munnetra Kazhagam (DMK), both during the 1970s; the Left-front parties; and Lok Shakti, during the 1980s—all demanded, in varying language, that the issue of centre–state relations be revisited. Besides their position on the issue of federalism, all these parties had a common political adversary—the Congress party—which was ruling at the centre when these parties were in power. In other words, in addition to the contested issue of federal relations, this represents anti-Congress politics also.

Intra-state Regional Politics

Region also becomes salient in politics within the states. The economic development of states often impacts the role of region. States like Gujarat and Maharashtra are comparatively more developed, thus offering greater employment opportunities to both semi-skilled and even less-skilled employment seekers. In any case, development has a gravitating effect and large-scale migrations often take place from less developed areas to the more developed parts—both within and across states. While such movement of population is unavoidable, the social and political effects, too, are unavoidable. Mumbai has for long been a city hosting diverse populations of workers and tradespeople coming to the city from far-flung places across the country. After a Marathi-speaking state of Maharashtra was formed in 1960, with Mumbai as its capital, political pressure began to build on the question of non-Marathi job seekers. A 'nativist' organization, Shiv Sena, emerged and began to mobilize the public on the issue of 'sons of soil'. While the Shiv Sena has been active in the politics of Maharashtra for over half a century, the phenomenon of nativist organizations is not an isolated development in Maharashtra alone. In Karnataka, too, an organization called Kannada Chaluvaligaru became active around the same time (in 1966) in Bangalore (now Bengaluru). The issue of outsiders in Assam is much more complicated than these two instances, but it is interesting to note that exactly about the same time, a 'sena' emerged in Assam, too, by the name of Lachit Sena, with the aim of fighting the influence of outsiders. This emergence occurred because, besides the 'outsiders' coming from across the border, Assam also faced migration by Bengali-educated and Bihari and Odiya unskilled job seekers eyeing employment in Assam's tea plantations. Thus, while resisting the inflow

47

of workers from other states, politics in many states evolved a regionalist flavour, with state governments expected not only to protect local job seekers, but also to uplift and support the development of local culture and language. Even in states like Kerala or Odisha, where manifestly nativist political movements did not shape, politics over governmental patronage to local culture and language always constituted a crucial element of regionalist politics. Having created many states on the basis of regional pride, it was only natural that politics in the states would have to engage with issues of nativism, regional culture, and language, and thus consolidate the regional pride that in the first place constituted an important element in the formation of the state.

Region as a factor in organizing politics manifests itself in one more way. While pride in the region and its language constitutes an important factor vis-à-vis outsiders, that same factor is inadequate in cementing internal cracks and competition within the state. Almost the same processes that contribute to the formation of a state also operate to challenge the unity and viability of the state. Thus, contestations *within* the state on the basis of intra-state regional sentiment shape and influence the politics of the state. In many large states, this happens due to the trajectory of development policies and their implementation. Parts of the state come up with a complaint of neglect. This complaint often relates to differential development of intra-state subregions. While this is expressed mainly in terms of regional backwardness, this politics refers to the political economy of development—in state after state, some parts allegedly receive more funding, more attention, and more share in power compared to other parts of the state. Both in objective terms and in terms of perception, some regions are backward compared to the state as a whole and compared to some (more developed) parts of the state. Sometimes, this is understood in terms of subregionalism, while the more common description is regional backwardness. Practically everywhere, from Jammu and Kashmir in the north to Tamil Nadu in the south and Assam and West Bengal in the east to Gujarat and Maharashtra in the west, echoes of regional 'imbalance' reverberate and mark newly emerging dynamics of politics at the state level.

In Jammu and Kashmir, Jammu region has always felt a stepmotherly treatment from the Kashmir-dominated political elite and its Kashmir-centric policies; in West Bengal, Darjeeling region is seen as backward; in Gujarat, Saurashtra region nurses a sense of injury just as in Maharashtra, Marathwada and Vidarbh regions are seen as more backward; in Karnataka, Bombay Karnataka and Hyderabad Karnataka both complain of backwardness. These examples can be listed from each state, but more particularly from the relatively larger states. The issue of backwardness or skewed development within a state takes various political expressions. At a most drastic level, such sentiments ignite the demands for separation from the parent state and formation of a new state, as it happened in the case of Telangana. Secondly, they force new constitutional and institutional arrangements such as autonomous district councils (Karbi Anglong Council in Assam), or autonomous regions (Bodoland in Assam, Gorkhaland in West Bengal, and so on), or statutory development boards (as in Maharashtra). Thirdly, and more commonly, these sentiments also throw up political solutions. Typically, ruling parties shuffle their leadership by bringing in a chief minister from the aggrieved region. This automatically also contributes to intra-elite alternation. Such changes also impinge on the nature of party support. In the aggrieved regions, either new political forces emerge or the pattern of party support changes. Besides, the issue of regional representation and development can easily become the basis for intra-party factionalism. Thus, the issue of intra-state imbalance often leads to political consequences that are relevant to party politics.

As these examples indicate, the trend is more in the direction of subregionalization of political consciousness. The experience of Tamil Nadu is perhaps very instructive in this regard. Even before Tamil Nadu in its present form came into being, a movement for the assertion of Dravid/Tamil identity shaped the political consciousness of the people speaking Tamil language. Once the non-Tamil speaking areas were separated from the erstwhile Madras state, the regional–linguistic consciousness of the Tamil-speaking areas became more pronounced, but took the form of anti–north India and anti-Hindi stance. This facilitated the continuation of the politics of Tamil regional identity in the Tamil-speaking state of Tamil Nadu. The DMK government (1967–72) was able to appropriate this regional legacy by initiating a debate over the issue of regional autonomy through the appointment of a committee (Rajmannar Committee). Even after the formation of the separate state of Madras, regional-ism remained a vital factor in the politics of Tamil Nadu. Thus, Tamil Nadu, like Maharashtra, represents instance of states where regional identity continued to constitute political consciousness even after the formation of a separate state. And yet, in the post-2000 period, cracks in the Tamil identity began to appear when demand for a separate state for the small region in the state, called Kongu Nadu, emerged. This demand is not yet politically very strong or salient, but its rise indicates that no large state is immune to the possibility of subregionalization of politics in the state. While this subregionalization is more common for large states, smaller states are not devoid of the possibility of further fragmentation of political consciousness on subregional lines. This is so because the idea of region (and subregion) draws strength from many factors, and just as language and dialect are one set of such factors, ethnicity, too, constitutes a basis for shaping regional identity. This is exemplified by the demands for separate Bodoland in Assam or demands for division of Meghalaya on the basis of ethnicity.

Regional Parties

If regions (and subregions) constitute bases of politics, it is only natural that groups and parties would form on those bases. It is mentioned earlier in passing how 'senas' were formed in different parts of the country— groups that call themselves 'armies' (in the regional cause). They are characteristic of political mobilizations on the basis of militant regionalism. There have also been sustained political movements for the regional causes. The Jharkhand movement has had a long history just as the movement for the Marathi-speaking state of Maharashtra went on for over a decade. These developments naturally led to crystallization of political groups identifying specifically with the regional cause.

Thus, some regional movements subsequently became political parties and began competing for power at the state level. The TRS, Jharkhand Mukti Morcha, and Uttarakhand Kranti Dal are examples of parties that emerged from state-formation movements. But even after a state has come into being, state-level parties have emerged and have gained popularity. Shiv Sena in Maharashtra is a case in point. It was formed in 1966, six years after the Marathi-speaking state was formed. (Though, of course, Shiv Sena did not succeed much in the politics of the state so long as it was exclusively relying on regionalist appeal. Its expansion coincided with its broadening of the political programme and adoption of Hindutva.)

One of the earliest instances of parties relying on regionalist agenda happens to be that of the DMK. (Other examples in this category could be AD and Jammu and Kashmir National Conference. However, in the case of the former, regional identity was inextricably mixed with language and religion, while for the latter, the struggle against the princely ruler combined with its early politics. In any case, the Dravid movement led by Periyar preceded the formation of National Conference.) During the pre-Independence period, a movement for the assertion of Dravid culture and identity took shape through the 1920s, and this legacy of the Dravid movement was turned into political capital by one of its leaders, C. Annadurai, when he formed the DMK in 1949. The party, and subsequently its breakaway faction, the All India Anna Dravida Munnetra Kazhagam (AIADMK), formed in 1972, successfully tapped regional sentiments and combined politics of regional identity with sustained mobilization on various other issues. Thus, the nexus between politics of regional identity and party politics has remained relevant in Tamil Nadu for the past seven decades.

In a vast country like India, it is only natural that political parties would emerge on the basis of region and/or parties would confine themselves to a particular region or state. In fact, there is a close relationship between states becoming main theatres of politics and the formation and rise of regional or state-based parties. Immediately after Independence, the idea of national freedom combined with the prominence of towering leaders of national movement created an impression that politics happens (mainly) at the all-India level. Even among students of Indian politics, this understanding predominated. Many political actors, too, believed in this. Therefore, many parties formed immediately after Independence aimed at becoming 'all-India' in scope. But a careful look at politics of the 1960s in retrospect, shows that each state was throwing up different patterns of local competition, there were new sets of state-level leaders emerging in each state, and in many states, state-level parties were beginning to emerge. All these parties did not necessarily emerge from a pre-existing regionalist approach.

Besides regional identity, two factors were responsible for the rise of state-based parties initially in the 1960s. Both were related to the history of Congress dominance. Around 1967, the Congress party became unable to hold together various factions and leaders under a common umbrella. The unity of disparate factions under the force of nationalist movement and, later, under the leadership of Nehru began to crumble as time passed. Those factions and leaders who found that they did not have enough freedom within the Congress began to distance themselves from the party and formed their own parties—often at the state level, since their support base would always be somewhat limited geographically and even socially. Even an attempt by a relatively more influential leader from Uttar Pradesh, Charan Singh, to form a nationwide party ended up in being a party restricted mainly to Uttar Pradesh. So, the post-1967 period witnessed the rise of Bangla Congress (1960), Kerala Congress (1964), and Jana Congress in Odisha (1966), among others.

A related political development further enhanced the rise of 'regional parties'. In the elections between

1952 and 1967, no single party was able to emerge as a strong competitor to the Congress party across states. The challenge to the Congress party could emerge only at the level of states and through parties that were confined to the state. In 1967, in many states, the Congress was unable to win clear majority, but no other party could do the same on its own. As a result, both Congress and non-Congress parties had to enter into alliances with other parties, including state-level parties, in order to form government. This situation had already occurred in Kerala earlier, and in 1967, it became characteristic of many more states. This window of political uncertainty gave state parties a crucial advantage. Therefore, just as many Congress factions converted themselves into separate parties, non-Congress political groups, too, took the form of parties at the state level. Not all these parties were regionalist. But many parties that restricted their operation to one state came into being in the wake of the 1967 elections. Thus, while it is true that in the period after 1984 state-based parties became much more important in India's politics than before, the phenomenon of regional or state-based parties is not new. (This discussion has somewhat loosely used the terms regional parties and state-based parties. For a detailed discussion on the nomenclature of these parties limited to one state, see Palshikar 2013.)

From the mid-1980s, a new phase in the life of regional and state-based parties emerged. The formation of Telugu Desam Party by the popular Telugu film star N.T. Rama Rao and that of Asom Gana Parishad as a follow-up of the long drawn movement against 'outsiders' in Assam (in 1985), marked this new phase. During the 1990s, many new state-based parties came into being. Like in 1967, this time, too, the inability of the Congress to hold together its state-level leaders and the inability of the Janata Dal (JD) to become an all-India force opposing the Congress led to the formation of a large number of state parties. Thus, the mid-1990s saw the rise of many parties originating in the Congress (such as Tamil Maanila Congress in Tamil Nadu, Trinamool Congress in West Bengal, and Nationalist Congress Party in Maharashtra). This period also witnessed emergence of many state parties from breakaway groups of the JD (Lok Shakti in Karnataka, Biju Janata Dal or BJD in Odisha, Samajwadi Party or SP in Uttar Pradesh, Rashtriya Janata Dal or RJD in Bihar, and so on).

Since the mid-1980s, three things changed as far as the politics of state-based parties is concerned. One, the number of regional parties and their representation in national legislature increased. (Between 1952 and 1984, it was only in 1984 that the seats won by parties not functioning at the all-India level went up to 79, that is, more than 14 per cent of seats in Lok Sabha. After 1985, only in 1989 and 1991 did this proportion go down to around 8 per cent—44 and 49 seats, respectively. Since then, the average share of such parties in the Lok Sabha has been 28 per cent seats—35, 34, and 31 per cent, respectively—but in 1998, 1999, and 2004, this was much higher.) Two, the role of state parties in forming the national government became critical. For the first time in 1989, state parties were critical in the formation of the central government as partners in the National Front. Since then, all governments at the centre have been coalition governments in which state parties are important members. (The National Democratic Alliance [NDA] government led by Modi that came to power in 2014 was the first government since 1989 that did not require a coalition and, thus, was independent of support from state-based parties. However, the Bharatiya Janata Party [BJP] did not abandon its allies; it continued with the tradition of coalition governments and included its partners in the ministry.) The period of 1996–2009 was perhaps the most fruitful from the perspective of state parties given their importance in the United Front governments, NDA and the two governments of the United Progressive Alliance (UPA) from 2004 to 2014. Three, regional parties began taking strong positions on many non-regional and all-India issues. As state parties began to be critical to formation of central government, they also emerged as important stakeholders in a range of policy issues beyond regional interests. Not only did parties like the DMK or AIADMK and Trinamool Congress start taking active interest in foreign policy because of their interest in India's policy towards Sri Lanka and Bangladesh, respectively, state parties, like any other all-India party, developed interest in policies regarding the economy, welfare programmes, and the like. In other words, the 'state' parties now became so only in the sense of their area of active operation, but in all other respects began to resemble so-called national or all-India parties.

These developments did not necessarily take place because regional consciousness suddenly increased after 1990; these changes occurred mainly as a result of the changing nature of politics in the country. These are all characteristics of the post-Congress polity. At the same time, these changes made states much more relevant to democratic mobilizations than before. Even when a party did not emerge on a regionalist platform, because its operations are confined to only one state, at some point or the other, every state party tends to take recourse to regionalist appeal and thereby enhances the relevance of region as a basis of political competition. For instance, a party like Trinamool Congress did not originally emerge on the basis of Bengali regionalism.

But because it was engaged in a bitter battle with the Left front government in the state, it had to concentrate on state-level issues, and, subsequently, when it was in direct confrontation with the Modi-led central government, the party could easily argue that attack on its government was anti-Bengali. Similarly, Bihar-based party Janata Dal (U) slipped into a Bihar-centric campaign in the assembly elections of 2015. Thus, during the period of Congress domination, regionalism provided the bulwark for organizing state level parties; in contrast, in the post-Congress phase, the proliferation and increased importance of state parties has helped further augment regional pride and regional consciousness.

Regional Challenges

So far the expressions of regional identity and demands that normally fall within the framework of electoral democracy to accommodate them have been reviewed. But sometimes, the politics of regional identity takes a more confrontationist stance and grows into a movement for separate national political identity. Such demands put severe pressure on the 'stateness' of the Indian state and push it into resorting to a militarist solution of the problem of militancy and secessionism. Yet open democratic contestation and efforts to negotiate such 'separatist' identities constitute the crux of democracy. On the one hand, protagonists of such 'separatist' demands would often claim that the demand represents popular sentiment in a particular region—and hence constitute democratic expressions of local population. On the other, liberals would wish that such demands are addressed in a 'democratic' manner and not suppressed; at the same time, such demands may have a cascading effect leading to similar demands from some other regions thereby bringing pressure and strain for the nation, and, finally, such demands also invite the use of state repression when they begin to challenge the formal state framework. Thus, separatist demands or demands for recognition of nationhood of any particular region are a challenge to both national- ism and democracy.

In the period right after Independence, some tentative demand for a separate Dravid nation was articulated. However, it soon subsided. Since then, such demands have occurred in the regions of the North West and North East. Even at the time of making of the Constitution, demands for separate national iden- tity did occur in Punjab, Kashmir, Manipur, Nagaland, and other states. While some of these were simply postponed without adequate resolution, as in the case of parts of the North East, some were politically pacified, such as Punjab. Yet, during the 1980s, the demand for Khalistan did assume serious proportions. The story of Kashmir has many complex dimensions, but the central point is the demand of various groups in Kashmir Valley from time to time that Kashmir should be recognized as an independent entity—as Azad Kashmir. Similar demands have always arisen in the North East—particularly in Mizoram (led by Mizo National Front), Nagaland (steered by various factions of the National Socialist Council of Nagas demanding Greater Nagalim), Manipur, and, of late, Assam (through the United Liberation Front of Assam or ULFA). In the case of Kashmir, a solution was sought through constitutional mechanism of Article 370. This solution has worked at times and has been rendered ineffective at some other times. It is alleged that the Government of India has not implemented the Article (giving full internal autonomy to Jammu and Kashmir), but some groups in the Kashmir Valley go beyond that to argue that they do not want to remain within the constitutional framework because they seek complete freedom from India. In the case of the Punjab and Mizoram, the Government of India combined the military solution with political negotiations leading to the Punjab Accord (1985) and the Mizo Accord (1986). Unfortunately, the Punjab Accord has not been implemented satisfactorily, yet Punjab has witnessed normal politics since 1991—after a gap of almost a decade. In Mizoram, the peace accord seems to have worked well, and insurgency has effectively subsided since it was signed. In the case of the Naga question, the Government of India has not been successful in arriving at a negotiated solution, although many rounds of negotiations have taken place between the government and the Naga rebel leadership. In 2015, a framework for peaceful talks was formally agreed upon, though the full settlement of the main issue is still pending.

It is necessary to note that such demands for political independence often bring about one inevitable effect. While supporters of the demands claim that the demands represent a democratic expression of the concerned people, the resort to violence by the insurgents means that the state machinery is left with little option but to use force. This has resulted in the controversial legislative measure called the Special Powers Act, which gives extraordinary powers to the Armed Forces when a particular area is declared as 'disturbed' area. First used in the Naga region, this provision has been used by the Government of India in Kashmir, Punjab, and Manipur. Such provisions have the effect of further keeping the people out of routine political processes—suspension of democratic politics.

These instances are instructive for a variety of reasons. In the first place, they show that democracy has sensitized our institutional framework to the need to adopt an 'asymmetric' approach to the federal arrangement. But more pertinent is the lesson that accommodation of some extraordinary regional demands needs to be seen as part of the democratic process. Various governments have accepted that a negotiated settlement is the only real solution to such 'separatist' demands. It is implicit in this approach that regionalist expressions are seen as having a different trajectory from other regions, and, therefore, in some regions while the demand for political independence is unacceptable to the Indian state, popular dissent and dissatisfaction are seen as part of democratic process. These examples remind us of three things. One, politics of regionalism has sometimes taken the complex route of separatism; two, separatist demands have quite routinely been accommodated through negotiation; and three, not suppression, but an open expression and recognition of regional sentiment, has been a more dependable and democratic way of handling such complications with some success.

The stressful experience of such separatist demands has made a deep impact on India's democracy. While the accommodation of such demands has enriched democratic capabilities, the use of violence (both by the 'separatists' and by the state) has simultaneously corroded democratic space.

This chapter has mapped the politics of regionalism as one instance of how democratic politics unfolds.

As already noted, politics of regionalism and regional demands often produce a new set of elite based in the regions. This development can be seen not only as inevitable, but welcome in terms of diversifying the composition of the political elite in the country, a necessary step in democratizing the political sphere. This change facilitated the diversification of the representational space: not only did the social composition of the elite undergo a change because of regionalization, it also brought about a change in issues and ideas that came to be represented in national politics. The elite coming from the backgrounds of region-based politics were also instrumental in shifting the agenda of politics to the issues dear to the regions.

However, region-based politics and rise of region-based elite did not necessarily bring about a change in the nature of politics in the regions. Politics in India's states did not become more democratic or more representative or more people-oriented only because of the emphasis on regions. Within regions, local patterns of domination continued to prevail and thrive. Thus, regional politics helped shape democratic mobilizations; at the same time, it helped sustain elite domination.

4

Democracy in Search of Well-being

Just as democracy encourages mobilizations and contestations, it is notorious for also evolving consensus. Critics of representative democracy often rue the fact that democracy leads to consensus and thereby produces closures. In a predominantly underdeveloped country like India, the issue of development can simultaneously be a matter of deep contestation and also a matter of overall agreement. There would be sharp differences over the routes to be adopted for development and there cannot be but an agreement on the urgency of development as a goal. Whether it is the language of development in early post-Independence India, or that of *garibi hatao* in 1971, or of *achche din* in 2014, parties and policymakers have always talked of larger visions to bring well-being to the ordinary men and women of India. In this sense, democratic politics has certainly evolved a broad agreement that the outcome of politics must be improvement in the life situation of ordinary citizens.

Underneath the apparent consensus on the question of development, however, politics is full of disagreements and differences on what constitutes development, how to achieve development, and who the chief beneficiaries of development would be.

In the 1950s, the socialist parties often chastised the Congress governments for not following adequately the socialist promise. The Congress party, on its part, adopted 'socialistic pattern of society' as its goal at its convention at Avadi in 1955. Subsequently, under Indira Gandhi's leadership the party claimed to be following a more explicitly socialist programme. Similarly, from time to time, groups and parties have emerged on the political scene which take pro-agriculture stance and claim that they are serving the interests of the rural sections vis-à-vis the urban population (which numerically continues to be much less—even by 2011, not even one in every three Indians was an urban dweller). Occasionally, some groups and organizations have agitated on behalf of the unorganized workers in the informal sector of the economy, but this has not given rise to any viable political force. The crux of these contestations has been the different understanding of what constitutes well-being and what constitutes the best way of bringing about well-being.

Right from the time of India's national movement, different ideas about development began to shape. Already in the 1920s, the Communist Party had emerged aiming to bring about a revolution by the working class (on the basis of the Marxist principles). In fact, the Marxists held that freedom in 1947 was only transfer of power from the British to the Indian bourgeoisie, and the task of real revolution—economic and political—was yet to be accomplished. They refused to participate in the making of the Constitution and in the immediate post-Independent period, a peasant uprising took place in Telangana region led by the Communists. Simultaneously, through the 1950s to the 1970s, the Left-led trade unions often forced the government to take into account the interests of the industrial workers and government employees. The trade union activity many times resulted into prolonged strikes by the unions.

Influenced by the Marxist dream, but not happy with the way the communists understood Marx, the socialists emerged as a distinct group around the mid-1930s. They initially identified themselves as 'Congress Socialists' because in the mid-1930s, when this group came into being, they were all participating in the national struggle for freedom under the auspices of the Congress party. Later, they increasingly became uncomfortable because of the disinterest the party organization displayed towards their ideas and programmes. Finally, they formed a separate 'socialist' party in 1948, when the Congress pushed them out by declaring that there cannot be 'party within party'. The socialists advocated active state control over the economy, including 'nationalization' of most industries and means of production. This was also the larger vision of Dr Ambedkar who named his early political party as Independent Labour Party. In the constitutional plan for free India that he had published in 1948 (*States and Minorities*), before joining the Drafting Committee of the Constituent Assembly, Ambedkar dwelt at length on the scheme of state control of major resources. Thus, in the immediate post-Independence period, Left and socialist politics was seen as a major alternative to the Congress party.

Shaping of the First Consensus

Differences between the ruling Congress party and opposition parties over various aspects of economic development did exist in the post-Independence period. But the period was characterized by the imprint of one particular imagination. There was a near consensus on the pre-eminence to be accorded to industrial development, and agricultural performance was seen as a crucial factor feeding into this larger scheme of things. The state was expected to regulate private interests on behalf of the public interest. This consensual understanding spanned the dominant thinking among intellectuals, policymakers, administrators, and political elite (majority of whom ironically came from agricultural backgrounds). The Congress party under Nehru's leadership came to represent this imagination. In this scheme of things, industrial development became the backbone of development as a project. Similarly, it was a matter of overall agreement during the early post-Independence period that the state had to play a central role in bringing about desired economic development.

The idea of proactive state in managing development was part of that consensus. It was believed that state represents the interests of the citizens (the public interest)—more so in a democratic context. Second, the dominant thinking believed that private players were not likely to work for the poor because of the profit motive with which they work; therefore, the state had to take up the responsibility of redistribution of resources and running of the welfare programmes by exercising control over private interests. Third, and at a more pragmatic level, it was also felt that in an economy marked by poverty and underdevelopment, the state alone can undertake huge investments and run the risk of late profits—particularly in the case of heavy industry and infrastructure. Thus, while there was indeed a democratic socialist tinge to the consensus, part of this consensus was also subscribed by the big capitalists of that time. This is famously reflected in the Bombay Plan that was formulated on the eve of Independence by a group of leading industrialists. This consensus was expressed through the more general framework of planning, public sector, and the mixed economy model.

Nehru was seen as the political architect of this consensus because of his moral authority with the bourgeoisie and political popularity to convince all sections of the masses, particularly the agricultural interests, that industrial development held the key to India's rapid economic advance. This framework also came to be known as state-controlled economy (or command economy). During the phase dominated by Indira Gandhi between 1966 and 1976, proactive state came to be criticized for its tendency to indulge in Licence-Permit-Quota Raj and the consequent degeneration into rent seeking among both the politicians and the bureaucrats.

Parties like the Bharatiya Jan Sangh (formed in 1951) and Swatantra Party (formed in 1959) were not fully convinced of this consensus. The control over private industrial interests was seen by them as negating 'freedoms' and/or impeding rapid industrialization. While both parties never managed to gain enough popularity, they represented the viewpoint different from the Congress-dominated consensus.

The Agrarian Challenge

The politically salient challenge to the consensus, however, came from those who believed that agriculture needed greater attention and a better deal. Their argument was based on the assumption that India was predominantly an agrarian society and also that agriculture could ensure greater livelihood opportunities in the society. Supporters of this viewpoint were sceptical of the policy of rapid industrialization. Charan Singh was the most vocal leader of this way of thinking. After trying to persuade the Congress to adopt pro-agriculture policies, he finally left the Congress party (in 1967) and formed the Bharatiya Kranti Dal (BKD) and subsequently the Bharatiya Lok Dal (BLD). His main base was among the farmers of Uttar Pradesh who mostly came from the Jat community (though he chose to present his case more as a pro-farmers policy). His departure from the Congress party was, of course, not only on the issue of agricultural policy; the factionalism in the Uttar Pradesh Congress party played an important part in Charan Singh's decision to form a separate party.

This was also the time when a small but influential section of the middle peasantry had begun to emerge mainly in north India. This section constituted the main base of Charan Singh and his rhetoric against industrialization. In a sense, as the traditional rural economy was coming under stress from industrial expansion, a new social cleavage was shaping in parts of the country: industry versus agriculture. This was not an entirely new development because at the time of making of the Constitution, this debate was already present. Just as democratic competition unfolded in pre-Independence period, the relatively better-off farmers who gained entry into the Congress had already got themselves entrenched in the party organization. Some sections of landlords and rich farmers, wary of the Congress's socialist rhetoric, always remained aloof from the party. Once the logic of democratic politics was further expanded after Independence, many rich farmers and landlords especially from north India chose to join the Congress and used their social status to win elections for the party. This made them important for the party. Elsewhere, like in Odisha, Rajasthan, and Gujarat, the landlords aligned with the erstwhile rajas and maharajas under the auspices of the Swatantra Party. Through the 1960s, the rich farmers who were slowly gaining ground, thanks mainly to the Green Revolution, grew more politically important in many parts of rural India and, at the same time, suffered from government's pro-industry policy. Charan Singh's political clout represented this section of the farmers who were not necessarily 'landlords', but were markedly well-off, who mostly belonged to the 'middle', both in terms of their landholdings and in terms of their caste status (as they were not exactly backward, but were also socially and economically distinct from the Thakur–Kshatriya communities), and thus they could have links both to the upper and lower echelons of the society. This location made the middle farmers the natural claimants for political power, as also the possible agents for the Congress (and later for the other parties) to mobilize rural constituencies for electoral support.

Charan Singh's followers kept on supporting him when he was in the Congress and even later, when he embarked on a series of political manoeuvres against the Congress. In fact, he and his social base in Uttar Pradesh constituted the bulwark of 'anti-Congressism' during his life time and even after his death. Charan Singh represented the interests of the middle farm-ers in the main. But the caste dimension of his social base cannot be easily brushed aside. Outside of Uttar Pradesh, he had very limited following, and in the

74

state, too, particularly outside the Jat belt of its western part, Charan Singh's appeal was only limited. He never succeeded—nor attempted—in creating a social base that extended to south India. In this sense, while Charan Singh represented the idea of agriculture, it is difficult to claim that he really represented the farmers in different parts of India. What his politics really represented were the three, sometimes overlapping, factors: agrarian interests (with prominence of middle farmers), middle castes, and the growing disenchantment with the Congress resulting in the politics of non-Congressism.

Farmers' Movements

While Charan Singh chose to operate through a separate political party since his departure from the Congress, many other important organizations working for the protection of agrarian interests also emerged in states ruled by the Congress, such as Karnataka, Maharashtra, Gujarat, and others. Their overall stance vis-à-vis urban industrial sector was best articulated by Sharad Joshi (though there was no agreement among them on the role of the state and the question of liberalization of economy). Sharad Joshi's Shetkari Sanghatana shot to prominence in the late 1970s in Maharashtra through its successful mobilization of the middle farmers of

Maharashtra on the question of remunerative prices for cash crops. Besides the phenomenal success that the Shetkari Sanghatana achieved in terms of huge following across castes among the middle farmers of Maharashtra, its arguments occupied important position in public debates because of the issue of 'terms of trade' between agriculture and industry, which Sharad Joshi raised both convincingly and evocatively. What made the Sanghatana politically significant was also the fact that for the first time in Maharashtra the agricultural interests were being mobilized effectively outside the Congress fold.

Though Sharad Joshi later shared the political space of north India with Mahendra Singh Tikait's Bharatiya Kisan Union (BKU), the larger alliance of agricultural interests could not take shape. Shetkari Sanghatana lost momentum by the late 1980s and Tikait's politics got subsumed within the more complex dynamics of Jat politics of western Uttar Pradesh. The overall rise of multiparty regionalized politics of the 1990s meant that state-specific mobilizations of farmers did not have much separate impact on electoral politics or on overall policies.

In a sense, politics based on the 'industry versus agriculture' divide always remained weak or peripheral. Why was this so? While agriculture, as distinct from industry, does constitute a major sphere of the economy for purposes of policy and more so for the purpose of political mobilization, 'agriculture' is a somewhat vague term. It hides more than it reveals. The agricultural sector has to cope with four divisions. There are landless farm labourers about whom, for instance, the farmers' movements allegedly never talk. They constitute a distinct class interest at the bottom of the class hierarchy. The politics of this class sometimes takes a more radical turn through Maoism. But in terms of electoral politics, this section is often taken for granted by parties and political leaders. Within the framework of competitive politics, it is not easy to identify any phase or party that specifically attended to the issues of landless agricultural labourers. At the other extreme are the rich farmers and large landlords whose interests are not in the agrarian sector as such since they have diverse interests such as moneylending, real estate, trade, and even industry. So, they are less likely to support the politics over agrarian interests. Then there is the middle farmer that emerged mainly due to the development strategies of the Indian state in post-Independence period. As seen earlier, this segment often gets represented in political parties, and, in fact, leadership in many states till very recently came mainly from this class of middle peasantry. And fourth, the numerically larger section consists of the small and marginal farmers who hold mostly dry land and are often beset with debts and penury. Of these four, the third section constitutes the middle peasantry castes and the fourth is often subsumed in the OBC category. This separation on the basis of caste identity and caste interests, besides the stratification based on economic differentiation, further complicates the possibility of 'agrarian politics' or politics of rural–agricultural interests. The weaker sections, though numerically large, are difficult to mobilize, while the richer ones are not interested in separate organizations because their interests are mainly in building coalitions with the bourgeoisie.

Emergence of the Second Consensus

The consensus that emerged in the post-Independence period thus had two key elements: industrial development and state control. Through the reign of Indira Gandhi, the latter of these two became much more controversial. She herself began to move slightly away from the excessive reliance on state controls when she returned to power in 1980 after a brief break following the elections of 1977. After her assassination, Rajiv Gandhi, who took over both as party leader and as prime minister, took more concrete steps in not only encouraging renovation of the goal of industrial development by upholding new technologies, he also indicated a turn towards relaxing state controls. The decade of the 1980s thus marked an unannounced shift in the role of the state in presiding over economic development. This shift was partly expedited by the crisis that India's economy faced during 1989–91, leaving little choice to the government of the day but to begin the process of 'restructuring' the economy.

As the shift away from the previous consensus began to shape through the 1980s and more prominently the 1990s, there were sharp debates among intellectuals, much unease among political actors, and some ideological positioning among political parties. In the early 1990s, when the Narasimha Rao government of the Congress party formally announced a shift towards liberalization and globalization, many non-Congress parties (JD and its fragments) and the Left parties began to criticize the new policy as a departure from socialism and welfarist idea of the state. However, the prospect of an ideologically divided politics quickly evaporated when most parties indirectly began to subscribe to a new consensus—the consensus over what came to be called the 'new economic policy'. By the mid-1990s, most parties had toned down their anti-liberalization rhetoric and also acquiesced in the new policy framework at the state level. When they became partners in the short-lived United Front governments of 1996–8, they had neither the ideological courage nor the pragmatic policy space to upset the new policy framework.

Finally, when the BJP came to power in 1998 (leading the NDA), it went much more wholeheartedly into the second generation of economic reforms, thus confirming the second consensus over economic development issues. By then, state-level parties such as Telugu Desam and the DMK had already begun implementing the new economic policies in their respective states. The BJD also joined this group of parties when it came to power in Odisha. This consensus got further affirmation when the Left front government of West Bengal modified its own policies. By 2004, there was no political party with the political strength to consistently oppose the new policy when out of power and also to depart from it when in power. In this sense, the 10 years between 1989 and 1999 was the decade when the second consensus shaped.

This second consensus implied a greater autonomy for market forces and global financial trends, reduced state controls, and, therefore, greater role to private players in the process of development. Studies have shown how the political elite adapted to these changes over the decade of the 1990s and even later. A transformation in their approach to development paradigm would not have come about unless the political elite had the confidence to both retain their clientelist networks and their social constituencies. Curiously, the question of economic reforms was never a critical issue placed before the electorate in any parliamentary election. The policy changes were brought about during 1991–6 by the Congress government, but the preceding elections did not debate the changes, nor were these debated much in the 1996 elections either. Therefore, economic policy changed, as one scholar has put it, by way of 'stealth' and yet a consensus (among the political elite, the industrial bourgeoisie, and the bureaucracy) did shape on the issue.

The way in which economic policy changes came about tells something very significant about the relationship between political elite and India's democracy: during the period that is seen as the 'graveyard' of incumbent governments, politicians and parties were not sent to and were not afraid of being sent to the graveyard of political wilderness on account of economic policy changes that they were effecting. So, the broader puzzle remains: that parties have been able to pursue policies without specific mandate and parties have been able to de-emphasize or offset disenchantment arising from policies. In assembly elections of Gujarat in 2012, the manifesto of the BJP specifically referred to the aspirations of the 'neo-middle-class' and sought support on the basis of the development model implemented by the then state government. Following the success in that election, Narendra Modi used the same rhetoric during the campaign for the 2014 parliamentary elections. After the success in the Uttar Pradesh assembly election of 2017, he more explicitly mentioned his vision that the 'new India' must move away from doles and seek new opportunities. These developments clearly indicate the near-consensual nature of the idea that while state may spend on welfare, the bulwark of development lay in privately led economic initiatives.

Limitations of Competitive Politics

How is it that competitive politics in a poor country allows parties to subscribe to this new consensus? While the political elite in the period immediately following Independence were said to be autonomous of the dominant material interests the political elite post 1990 appear to be autonomous of the electorate itself. This peculiar situation can be understood in the context of at least four crucial features of competitive politics.

First, competitive politics and electoral politics in particular shapes primarily on the basis of the menu of choices offered. Through the 1980s, and more so during the post-1990 period, the menu regarding the policies related to development and well-being remained within the broader rubric of growth-oriented economic policies. Neither the Left nor the social justice parties of north India came up with any viable and different policy framework. Their criticisms were centred on ideological arguments and an adherence to the older approach of state controls. By the middle of the 1990s, even that criticism became tame in force and weak in vigour. State after state had to resort to soliciting foreign direct investments and compete with each other in bringing new industries and corporate investments in their states. Since, effectively, almost all parties were offering the same fare of policy choices, the parties and elite were insulated from the possibility of a competition on these issues and thus could manage to deflect or displace popular disenchantments on the immediate effects of new policies.

Second, this deflection could be possible because Indian democracy was simultaneously undergoing a period of social churning. People and parties alike were more concerned with two issues that tested India's democratic resilience. On the one hand, the issue of Hindu nationalism was agitating the country since late 1980s, and in many parts of the country a sharp religious polarization was shaping. On the other, the question of fair share for the backward castes in public employment and power emerged as the major cleavage at the same point in time. The deep in-roads these two issues made into the public mind during the crucial decade of 1989–99 meant that much of party politics and public debates centred on these two issues. Social schisms emerged on the 'communal' and the 'OBC' questions. Political polarizations, too, tended to base themselves on communal versus secular axis and/or the pro-Mandal versus anti-Mandal axis. In turn, issues of poverty, dis-privilege, and marginalization got defined in terms of caste and community and expressed in terms of social location.

Third, competitive politics for long had been beset with populist rhetoric. Ever since the rise of Indira Gandhi in late 1960s and early 1970s, the mainstay of politics was the ability to sway the masses with slogans, promises, and symbolisms. This tendency pushed aside all possibilities of an informed public discourse on available choices and their relative merits or applicability. The populist style of politics ensured that leaders and parties need not engage with ideas and policies in order to win public support; the ability to convince the public of the leader's or the party's lofty intentions was sufficient political capital. This long-standing feature practically insulated the elite from public scrutiny of policy preferences. It also meant politics centred on personalities and opposition to personalities rather than policies.

And fourth, family-centred politics of most state parties, too, makes it unnecessary for leaders and followers to connect to each other on the basis of policies and ideas of development. Once trust is posited in a family, followers do not have to examine the policies of the party because they would implicitly also trust the party and believe its policies to be beneficial to them. For the leader, too, it is sufficient to earn the trust of the followers on the basis of personal popularity and personal authority without going into the nitty-gritty of policy. The 1990s witnessed the growth in the popularity of regional or state-based parties and all such parties invariably revolve around one leader or one family. This feature allowed competitive politics to remain considerably aloof from intensive debates over policy alternatives.

Issue of Land Acquisition

During the course of the second consensus, the only major issue that has so far worried the policymakers has been that of acquiring land for various development and infrastructure projects. This issue has a long history of antagonism between the capitalist impulse of acquiring more and more land for industry and urbanization, on the one hand, and the complex issues of compensation and challenge to livelihoods of farmers, on the other. During the period of greater state control over the economy, the state was the main claimant of much land acquisition in the name of 'public interest', and, as such, the politics of land acquisition was mostly played out within the ambit of 'right to property', and the main theatre of that politics was the judiciary as opposed to the legislatures—the former arbitrating property rights and compensation issues, while the latter claiming authority over deciding what constituted public interest. As the post-1990 phase of liberalization of the economy began to unfold, the instrument adopted by the state for 'facilitating' rapid development (of industry and urban centres) shifted to special economic zones (SEZs). But the net result for ordinary landholders was the same: their lands would go, and while markets might result into some bargaining powers and better prices for land, nexus between state and capitalist classes meant that actual market prices could get manipulated considerably below the real market prices; and, most importantly, the alienation of land often endangered the livelihoods of the affected farmers in spite of various economic and employment packages. These issues ensured that there were organized and sporadic resistances to giving land for SEZs or for new development and infrastructure projects in many parts of the country. The violence that erupted at Nandigram in West Bengal in 2007 over the issue of SEZ is perhaps the most publicized controversy, but

SEZs have produced political protests in many other states as well.

While locally the parties in the opposition often used these occasions to mobilize people against the ruling parties, no party had any clear position on the issue. Most agreed on the need to have SEZs and hence implicitly also agreed on the need to facilitate land transfers in favour of industry or infrastructure, but electoral compulsions meant that the parties took equivocal stand on the issue. In a sense, this was typical of the new consensus that was emerging through the 1990s on questions of 'new' economic policy in general. The issue of land acquisition assumed most serious proportions in West Bengal over the question of Tata Motors project of the Nano car to be situated at Singur. The Left-led government that wanted to facilitate this miscalculated the popular resistance to the policy, while the Trinamool Congress was prompt in mobilizing popular protests against this project, finally forcing the government to retract and the company to decide to move out of the state. The Singur case exemplifies the compulsions of the state government, desperation of the landholders, and political advantages gained by political rivals, all of which would play a role in the politics of land acquisition in particular and in the onward march of the second consensus more generally. Since land rights have been at the core of most development projects, industrial and infrastructure development becomes a controversial issue despite the prevailing consensus. While the response of state machinery has often been that of repression and bureaucratic collusion with private interests (as alleged in the Reliance SEZ at Raigad in Maharashtra), the government has also come up with some remedial legislation to protect land rights. The Forest Rights Act, 2006, and the Land Acquisition and Rights Act, 2013, were important steps at least on paper to recognize the need to adopt broader policy wisdom in this regard.

In fact, the issue of land makes both the moments of consensus quite vulnerable to popular disenchantment. But among the elite, there has been a firm agreement on the need to appropriate land without adequately ensuring a democratic process of negotiation. This elite consensus might appear almost as a seamless journey of the hegemonic takeover of the realm of development policies. However, in spite of such a consensus (and surely because of that), Indian democracy has had many punctuation marks in the smooth narrative of elite domination. Two such moments deserve a mention. They proffer arguments for greater popular control over resources and they also talk about more direct participation by people. However, they have many fundamental differences.

The Maoist Challenge

The first challenge, emanating from the Left, has its origin in the very early period of Independence. It revolved around the land question—or more specifically the issue of landlordism and redistribution of agricultural lands. Being a subject under jurisdiction of the states, 'land reform' ran into trouble because of the control exercised by landed interests over the ruling Congress governments on many states.

Even before the states could begin to frame policies regarding land reforms, violent struggles erupted on the land question. The peasants (and mostly landless agricultural labourers) led by communists in the Telangana region as also West Bengal (this was movement by the sharecroppers, known as the Tebhaga movement, for its demand that sharecroppers be obliged to hand over only one-third of the produce to the landowner instead of the mandated one-half share) were up in arms posing a challenge to the authority of the Indian state (in 1947). These uprisings were the first major challenge to democratic politics because of their use of violence and timing—well before the first general elections. Both necessitated the use of force by the newly independent state.

The questions that came to the forefront were: Is real social change possible in the framework of constitutional democracy? Can interests opposed to each other be mobilized within a democratic framework? Is it possible to organize the poor and deprived sections and push for policies in their favour by means of democratic practice? The Communist Party was arguing that answers to all these questions were definitely in the negative. Though the Communist Party later modified its stand on the possibility of democratic struggles within a constitutional framework, many of its more extreme cadres continued to have doubts about this and ultimately broke away from the party and engaged in revolutionary armed struggles. These rebels came to be known as the Naxals—the name is derived from the area Naxalbari in West Bengal, where, during the late 1960s, violent struggles were waged by young revolutionaries.

The Naxalite movement that emerged in late 1960s in West Bengal has subsequently spread into many parts of Bihar, Odisha, Chhattisgarh, and adjoining states of Madhya Pradesh and Maharashtra. As the various underground organizations running the struggles believe in the Leninist–Maoist interpretation of Marx's thought, these groups are known as Maoist groups. The areas where the Maoists have founded a base for themselves are very poor, backward, and most of these are dense forest areas inhabited mainly by the Adivasi populations. The utter deprivation and backwardness of these regions, in addition to continued efforts by both state governments and the centre to appropriate natural resources from these areas without adequate policies to ensure the protection of local populations and their habitations, have resulted into considerable support to the Maoist organizations in these regions. The success of Maoists in appealing to the Adivasis in particular signifies the mobilizational space available in these regions, while on the other hand, the resort to armed revolts and indiscriminate use of violence by the Maoist groups poses a challenge to democratic politics. In the course of the long history of the Maoist movement since late 1960s, there are also instances when some Maoist groups agreed to give up armed struggle and become part of the open political arena of democratic competition and even showed willingness to be part of the electoral process. Thus, the experience of Maoism, while indicating the difficulty that the open democratic process experiences when armed struggles emerge, also shows the deeper links between electoral mobilizations and mobilizations that shun the electoral arena because of the latter's tendency to compromise larger public interest and shrink to only formal power considerations.

Ironically enough, the Maoist insistence on using violence has meant that the entire issue has got converted into a 'law and order' problem and the core

matters of land distribution and democratic appropriation of natural resources have been almost completely
sidetracked in political party circles, while the Maoists
themselves, too, are mostly engaged in combating the
state apparatus to the exclusion of their core issues of
struggle. The Maoist appeal also fails in expanding to
the social sections beyond the very poor Adivasi communities. The Maoists have not been successful even
in mobilizing the large masses of landless agricultural
labourers in whose interests their struggles originally
began. So, here is an instance of politics stretching the
idea of democracy too far—in the process jeopardizing
democracy—by shaping a broad ideological platform
and yet failing to translate that platform into viable
politics either by popularizing it across social sections
or spreading it across states of India.

Challenge to 'Development Model'

The other moment of punctuating the prevailing elite
consensus is related to the long and peaceful struggle
waged by villagers displaced by the ambitious irriga-
tion projects on the Narmada river. While it began
as the protest against policy (or non-policy) of relief
and rehabilitation of the affected villages, the protest
grew into a robust critique of the idea of development
itself. Led by Medha Patkar under the auspices of the

Narmada Bachao Andolan, the movement became the node around which many other local struggles against 'development projects' can be placed. The Andolan argued about the rapacious and unjust—therefore undemocratic—nature of the accepted idea of development. It represented an alternative approach often referred to as 'sustainable' development that would take care of balance between nature and mankind besides also ensuring democratic process for deciding regulation and appropriation of natural resources. The movement adopted the routes of mass struggles by the affected villagers besides seeking judicial interventions. The major contribution of the movement has been in the field of ideas; while the movement succeeded in sensitizing policymakers to the issue of rehabilitation, it could not really dent the existing consensus over development. The movement is nevertheless important for the theoretical challenge that it poses for democracy and the discourse of well-being, for its ability to bring together the issues of sustainable development, authentic life style and environmentalism, and for deeply pricking the conscience of the middle classes (who nevertheless continue to subscribe to the consensus).

In the case of both Maoism and the movement for sustainable development, they emanated from specific protests and objections to the existing ideas of development and then grew into broader critiques having the potential for a more general appeal. But the experience of both is similar: political constituencies that get constructed through their appeal tend to be limited in the social and spatial expanse they occupy. As a result, the actual impact or capacity to intervene in ongoing processes remains deeply problematic.

5

Politics of Social Justice

Caste has always been a central question in India's politics. Claims about representation, share in power, and claims over welfare measures are often presented in terms of caste. The institutional design of free India—the Constitution—prohibits the most obnoxious manifestation of caste, that is, untouchability, and also guarantees equal treatment as a right.

The Constitution addresses the concerns of social inequality in three different ways. One, it provides for the reservation of seats in national and state legislatures for SCs and STs (Articles 330 and 332). Two, it empowers the state to undertake measures for the well-being of the backward classes (Articles 15 and 16). And three, it empowers the state to provide reservations in public employment in order to ensure that the backward classes are 'adequately' represented in the administration of the State [Article 16(4)]. Besides ensuring representation of certain backward communities in both politics and administration, these provisions have the potential of creating a politically important small class of elite among the backward communities—a class that would subsequently not only demand greater share in power, but also mobilize the masses from those social sections.

Awakening among the backward castes has led to three interdependent processes: claims to affirmative action for the backward communities, rise of elite or leadership among these backward communities, and political assertion by the backward castes. These three are, in turn, responded to by the so-called upper castes by entering into political alliances. Thus, 'caste politics' refers to both the struggles by the backward castes to wrest a space in democratic politics and the efforts by the upper castes to minimize the impact of backward-caste politics and retain privilege. In this sense, caste politics touches upon the interests of the different sections of society and so long as such interests are linked to caste, caste politics is bound to occur within the framework of competitive politics. Besides material interests, caste often leads to a sense of identity for its members, and, therefore, caste politics also takes the form of politics of caste identity. Paradoxical as it may seem, the interface between democracy and caste produces two contradictory tendencies. On the one hand, it encourages castes to forge larger, multi-caste coalitions in order to become politically viable, while, on the other, it produces sharper identities of individual castes through caste associations and the calculations of numerical share of individual castes among the office holders.

While the language of social justice came to be employed much later, the core issues have consistently been present in India's politics not just after Independence, but for a long time before Independence also. Democracy and politics of social justice have a close and often symbiotic relationship: while the scope of democracy expands as a result of the politics of social justice, the spread of democratic logic and establishment of democratic institutions in turn ensures (is supposed to ensure) strengthening of the politics of social justice.

While the demands and claims of different communities for reservation policy are often played out at the institutional level through judicial arbitration, legislative deliberation, and policymaking, in the last instance, these are matters of democratic contestations in the public realm. Only through a combination of public discourse, legislative deliberation, and judicial arbitration do policies of affirmative action finally take shape. While the constitutional provision for SCs and

STs has acquired considerable consensus, the policy of reservations for the OBC did create a stiff public controversy during the late 1980s and early 1990s. Only after the judicial pronouncement in the Mandal case (Indra Sawhney Case, 1992) did the controversy gradually subside to give way to a consensus among political parties over both policy of OBC reservation and sharing of powers with the OBC. That consensus may be described as the moment of integration of the social justice agenda with democratic politics. However, such a consensus does not exclude the possibility of contested issues still awaiting democratic resolution. Of course, it would be inadequate to restrict the discussion of 'social justice' to only politics that surrounded reservation policy. The core of social justice agenda consists of power sharing among castes within an unequal society plagued by caste-based discrimination. Therefore, this chapter will mainly assess the capacity of India's democracy to accommodate diverse claims by different caste groups and tribal communities by looking at the political mobilizations that shaped over the past one century.

The latter half of the nineteenth century witnessed the early mobilization of the backward castes in the Marathi-speaking region inspired by the writings of Jyotirao Phule. During his lifetime and immediately after his death, Maharashtra witnessed the rise of awareness among the backward castes who organized as *satyashodhaks*, or seekers of the truth, and subsequently politically organized as the non-Brahmins. The project of bringing together all oppressed communities as 'non-Brahmins' thus began to shape in the early twentieth century. This coincided with similar collective mobilizations in south India under the influence of the Tamil social activist and politician Periyar Ramasamy Naicker. The early decades of the twentieth century (1920–40) witnessed the rise of anti-caste movement among the then untouchable communities under the leadership of Ambedkar. The period immediately after Independence, however, did not witness any explicit mobilization on caste basis nor the formation of specifically caste-based parties. In fact, Ambedkar prompted his followers to form a party that would seek to represent all sections of society rather than only one particular community.

Slow and Grudging Transformation

The decades of the 1950s and 1960s, nevertheless, witnessed one particular transformation in the pattern of power sharing: in many parts of the south and west, a new political elite belonging to the middle peasant castes emerged. They were often placed between the upper castes and the more backward 'lower' castes. This development had a long socio-historical context. The peasant castes that emerged as politically important had a tradition of landholding; the regions where this happened had weaker versions of landlordism in prevalence; the communities that gained political importance had begun to mobilize during early twentieth century itself; many of these were relatively better off as landholding communities; and above all, these communities, in many cases, had a numerically large presence in the regions where they now began to become dominant politically. In Tamil Nadu, for instance, the long decades of the anti-Brahmin movement had brought together many communities even before Independence. In Karnataka and Andhra Pradesh, the Lingayats and Reddis, respectively, were landowning communities and had a large presence as single communities. In Gujarat, the Patidar Kanbis similarly had numerical strength and deep roots in agriculture. In Maharashtra, besides being politically mobilized during the non-Brahmin movement and having a history of landownership, the Marathas also had the advantage of numerical strength across the state. As can be seen from these examples, the formation of linguistic states often helped these different communities to gain critical numeric presence—in the undivided Bombay state, neither the Lingayats nor the Marathas or Patidars would have that advantage. Similarly, Reddis of Andhra

Pradesh would not have the advantage in Madras state to which parts of Andhra belonged before a separate Andhra Pradesh was carved out.

In other words, the transformation that was taking place in some parts of India was a combined result of the history of mobilization, the specificity of agrarian relations, location in caste hierarchy, and the political context of state formation. Democratic political arrangements contributed to this transformation, but they alone might not have been sufficient to bring it about. Precisely for this reason, democratic arrangements being the same across the country, similar transformation did not occur everywhere. Only where democracy was combined with local socio-historic context and material condition of the concerned community, the 'democratic effect' was visible.

Politics over the share of different caste groups began to shape much more because of the failure of routine democratic processes to produce a change in many parts of India, notably, the north. By ordinary democratic logic, the composition of elite including the composition of the leadership of political parties should have changed simply because the so-called upper castes are often a hopeless minority in most parts of the country. But this logic did not automatically apply because of the material domination of the upper castes in most parts was accompanied with a resultant hegemonic hold over institutions and public opinion. In states like Uttar Pradesh, Bihar, and Odisha, the upper castes enjoyed greater control over resources—mainly through landownership—and also had slightly larger numeric presence than their southern counterparts. The anti-caste and non-Brahmin protests and uprising that marked parts of the south and west were also absent in the case of these regions. As a result, the backward castes had very little opportunity to benefit from the logic of democracy.

This reflected in the power equations in states like Uttar Pradesh, Bihar, Odisha, and Madhya Pradesh. Unlike in Maharashtra, Andhra Pradesh, Karnataka, or Tamil Nadu, where party and governmental leadership had shifted to the middle peasantry castes, in these states, the upper castes continued to control key public positions. The lack of previous history of mobilization, however, caused a diffuse response during the 1960s and even the next decade. As mentioned in the previous chapter, Charan Singh began to mobilize the 'middle peasants' (Jats) of Uttar Pradesh during the 1960s. The disappointment of these sections caused the Congress party's defeat in the belt that had remained aloof from the democratic transformation along caste lines. Of course, the immediate factor responsible for this was the attempted unity among non-Congress parties. But that surely was not the main reason; a somewhat loosely united opposition became the platform that facilitated the expression of disappointment and anxiety among the backward communities in these states.

The Congress under Indira Gandhi must have sensed this. In the following elections (parliamentary election of 1971 and assembly elections in most states in 1972), the Congress party decided to abandon its catch-all strategy and adopted a policy of exploiting the social cleavages along class and caste lines. Besides harping on the general theme of 'poverty' and thereby projecting itself as the saviour of the poor, it also sought to forge a social coalition of upper and very lower sections, the Dalits and Adivasis (besides Muslims). This, with Indira Gandhi's populist rhetoric, managed to keep the non-Dalit lower castes out of power and rendered them unable to control the course of politics.

But this strategy also had another fallout. The non-Dalit backward castes in north India kept their distance from the Congress and became a ready constituency for non-Congress politics. Socialists and Charan Singh's followers managed to strike deeper roots in parts of north India as a consequence. This was evidenced in 1977 when non-Congress parties came together to form the Janata Party, which received overwhelming support in north India. The defeat of the Congress Party at the all-India level ushered a new phase in competitive politics in the country; it also encouraged the non-Congress parties in further augmenting their social base. In Bihar, the Janata Party government decided to implement a new policy of reservations for the backward castes. This decision received fierce opposition from the upper castes, and while the government had to retreat, this development underlined the clear social divide obtaining there—between the 'forward' (*agada*s) and 'backward' (*pichhada*s). This also led to the appointment of the second backward classes' commission (popularly known as Mandal Commission, named after its chairperson). Both the Congress defeat of 1967 in states of north India and the opportunity for socialists and Charan Singh's followers to exercise power in 1977–8 facilitated the entry of a new political elite belonging to the backward and middle peasantry castes. This was deeply resisted by the upper castes, and north India continued to remain divided socially and politically despite the return of the Congress to power in 1980.

Towards 'Democratic Upsurge'

The next round of transformation began around 1990 when the short-lived government of V.P. Singh decided to implement the key recommendation of Mandal Commission relating to 27 per cent reservations for OBC in central government jobs and educational institutions. This was the moment when claims by OBC leaders such as Mulayam Singh Yadav, Sharad Yadav, Lalu Prasad, and others, became central to political contestations. This was also the time when some peasant OBC communities were in a position to organize behind these leaders. Thus, there existed a political constituency and also the political claimants to that constituency. This changed the nature of politics altogether. The developments that began in an embryonic form in the late 1960s had finally come to fruition.

As a matter of fact, the most critical changes happened only in the two states of Uttar Pradesh and Bihar. Some less dramatic, but important changes occurred in Madhya Pradesh as well. Basically, in social environments that were deeply agrarian and at the same time hierarchically structured the tension between democratic logic and logic of traditional power equations clashed, and the latter became weak to some extent giving way to new political configurations. However, given their size, these states have the capacity to change the texture of politics in the country as a whole, and the momentous changes occurring there quickly came to be recognized as a new phase— OBC politics. The term 'OBC' had by then become commonplace to refer to those castes that were listed as backward by the Mandal Commission. This new category now began to dominate the discourse of politics as well as actual political processes. But besides the states of north India in particular, the 1990s also witnessed some new features across the country as a whole, and these were captured in Yogendra Yadav's famous categorization as the 'second democratic upsurge'. Though there are many elements of this upsurge, the rise of political interest and awareness among the backward communities is a crucial element in shaping the upsurge. Javeed Alam provocatively argued that the poor and backward constitute the critical bulwark in favour of democracy. The political rhetoric of social justice employed by leaders emerging from backward-class backgrounds bore fruit, and the voters from the backward communities increasingly gravitated towards these leaders during the 1990s. So much so that parties like the SP and RJD came to be known as 'OBC parties'—they were OBC parties in the sense of their main agenda, their core following, and their clear preference for candidates belonging to backward-class backgrounds. This upsurge made a difference to the social composition of representatives in the two states that were lagging behind in the first democratic transformation of the 1960s.

This transformation did have limitations though. Even when the two most critical states were undergoing this transformation, states like West Bengal and

Odisha were still mostly untouched by the democratic upsurge in favour of the backward classes. Similarly, the state to have witnessed an early transformation, Maharashtra, did not participate much in the upsurge. Maratha domination of politics remained more or less intact and the dispersal of power beyond the Maratha community was only nominal. But, most importantly, in Bihar and Uttar Pradesh the transformation of the 1990s remained a severely narrow affair because it did not encompass the complex and diverse range of communities. Instead, benefits of the upsurge were captured mostly by one or two communities in both the states. Yadavs (and to some extent Kurmis in Bihar) rose to political prominence, and the OBC wave soon came to be identified as the rise of the Yadavs. In both states, the large number of 'more backward' communities continued to remain excluded from political and governmental power. Ironically, the politics that aimed at forging the political unity of the 'backward' communities produced a new split—between 'upper' OBC and 'lower' or 'more' backward OBC.

Phase of Consensus

By late 1990s, the issue of social justice ceased to be a contentious one. The policy of affirmative action (reservations) became acceptable to all parties. Similarly, acknowledging the political importance of the OBC, all parties began to accord space to the emerging political elite belonging to OBC backgrounds, and finally, parties also began to work hard to attract the OBC voters. Thus, a major change witnessed since 1999 was that parties competed with each other to show how they were true supporters of the cause of social justice. Thus, all parties had to recognize the logic of numbers so crucial in democracy. As party competition became more and more severe, parties needed to expand their electoral base by broadening their social constituency. Instead of OBC being supporters of any one party, OBC vote began to be divided among different parties and across different states.

The most striking example of this has been the change in the approach and social composition of the BJP. A party once derided by opponents as party of urban traders, middle classes, and upper castes, the BJP set out to change itself through what was once described by one of its leaders as 'social engineering'. The schism emerging among the OBC because of the Yadav-centric politics of the SP and RJD came in handy for the BJP. It went on to attract the 'lower OBC' in many parts of the country, especially in Uttar Pradesh, Bihar, and Madhya Pradesh. In 1999, the party was successful in gaining 20 per cent OBC votes across the country, and this same factor was further strengthened more dramatically in 2014 when it polled 34 per cent votes among the OBC (vote share figures based on National Election Study of 1999 and 2014, respectively). The Congress has consistently failed to win back the OBC voters in most parts of the country. But, in principle, all parties now recognize the importance of OBC votes, and many parties are even prepared to allow the elite from OBC background to share power within the party. In this sense, this third phase represents the stabilization of the rise of OBC as a political force and consensus among parties over sharing power with OBC.

While the foregoing story of the rise of OBC may be somewhat gratifying from the viewpoint of democratization of power, unless power is shared routinely with the more ostracized and socially and economically more marginalized communities, democratic transformation brought about by OBC politics would not be meaningful. What has been the record of democracy on this front? How has democracy ensured integration of the Dalits and Adivasis into the political process?

Dilemmas before Dalit Politics

Historically, politics of SCs, or Dalits, is faced with two sets of dilemma. The first dilemma has been about the choice of a political vehicle and the other about mode of politics. It involved relationship of Dalit masses with existing political forces. At the time of Independence, Congress happened to be the most popular party, but it was also a party that was dominated by upper castes in most states. So, going with such a party ran the risk of sidestepping key concerns of Dalits. Yet, because of the charisma of Nehru, and in north India because of the leadership of Babu Jagjivan Ram, large sections of Dalits (including Dalit activists and aspirants) supported the Congress in the immediate post-Independence period. On the other hand, across India, a sizable section among Dalits was deeply influenced by the thinking of Ambedkar. At the time of his death, Ambedkar had almost completed the process of forming the new political party, the Republican Party of India (RPI). Though the party was not imagined as working for Dalits only, it was clear that it would be specifically catering to the needs and political aspirations of the Dalit community, that it would follow Ambedkar's political ideas, and that it would be led by leaders coming from the Dalit community. The activists who were close to Ambedkar and who were convinced of his ideas mostly chose to join the RPI rather than any other party. But the RPI could never take off in the real sense. The public prejudice that it was only a party of Dalit community may have been a factor behind this, but the internecine factionalism and rivalry among

Ambedkar's followers neutralized whatever impact the RPI could have. Barring Maharashtra, whereas elsewhere, it was weak due to factionalism, soon the RPI ceased to be a political force of any importance, and, as a result, the vast energy generated by the Ambedkarite movement remained available for other parties to tap.

In the 1980s, Kanshi Ram rose to prominence arguing that all parties (but specifically the Congress and BJP) were equally callous about the Dalit question because they were under the influence of anti-Dalit ideas of *Manuwaad* (tendency to believe in the non-egalitarian ideas allegedly contained in the Manusmriti). He revived the idea that Dalits should have an independent political vehicle, but derided the faction-ridden RPI and formed a new political party, the Bahujan Samaj Party (BSP). While the party called itself the party of the *bahujan samaj*, that is, the majority community, it was pitched as a party of the Dalits (the OBC could join it, but Dalits would lead it). Initially, the BSP made in-roads in states like Himachal Pradesh, Haryana, Punjab, and in Delhi, besides Uttar Pradesh. But during its three-decade-old career, the BSP has been successful only in Uttar Pradesh in winning repeatedly the confidence of the SCs there.

One can therefore look upon the BSP as the second attempt at creating a separate vehicle of Dalit politics after Maharashtra. In Maharashtra, the limited share

111

of Dalits in the population, factionalism among RPI leadership, the limited sectional support gained by the RPI, and the dominance of the Congress party contributed to a very limited role of the RPI. It never seriously attempted to broad-base itself or attract the OBC voters. Only in the 1990s, a faction led by Prakash Ambedkar made an effort in that direction when it floated a party of the Bahujans—the Bahujan Mahasangh. Even in Uttar Pradesh, where the BSP has carved a place for itself, much would depend upon the nature of party competition and the ability of various parties to attract the OBC. In the parliamentary election of 2014, the BSP failed to make any impact and subsequently lost the Uttar Pradesh assembly elections of 2017 leading to a possibility that the party may lose its overall following elsewhere too. Therefore, the nagging question is whether 'Dalit politics' can shape in the form of a separate political party or as part of the overall party politics.

Party or Movement?

The other dilemma before Dalit politics pertains to the form of politics. Ambedkar combined electoral politics with struggles for the rights of Dalits. This gave rise to both politics of formal power and politics of movement and social change. When the RPI was formed, post-Independence electoral politics had already taken off. So, it was only natural that the RPI mainly focused on party politics, though it also actively participated in the movement for the formation of Marathi-speaking state of Maharashtra. Subsequently, one of its leaders, Dadasaheb Gaikwad, took the lead in organizing mass satyagrahas on behalf of the landless labourers. However, within the party this was seen as a deviation from the 'parliamentary line'. Thus, there was a tension between those who wanted to combine street struggles with electoral politics and those who wanted to confine the party only to electoral politics. In the late 1960s, a group of young firebrand activists from among the Dalit community began to restlessly oppose the parliamentarism of the leadership and developed a trenchant critique of that strategy as also of the established leadership. This group subsequently formed the Dalit Panthers—an organization that was dedicated to struggles as opposed to party politics. The 1970s witnessed the rising popularity of the Panthers among younger Dalits, and when the conflict broke out between caste Hindus and Dalits over giving Ambedkar's name to the Marathwada University in late 1970s, the Panthers were seen as the militant protectors of the Dalit interests and also the ones who could present a cogent intellectual argument against caste Hindus. However, soon, sections of the Panthers began to be attracted to party political arena and started joining some party or the other, many joining some RPI faction.

The Dalit Panthers have influenced the struggles of Dalits in Karnataka, Tamil Nadu, and Andhra Pradesh, among many other pockets. The Dalit parties of Tamil Nadu have been trying to combine the two strategies of people's struggles and intervention in party politics. Like Maharashtra, in Tamil Nadu also the numerical strength of the Dalits can just about allow them to be a small but critical force only at the time of political instability or coalition politics. Therefore, they have to resort to more radical protest activity from time to time. In Andhra Pradesh, in particular, many young Dalit activists joined the Maoist underground groups from time to time. This, too, was a step out of disillusionment with party politics and its corrupting effect on the agenda of social transformation. Kanshi Ram shot into prominence mainly through politics of movement through his firebrand platform, the DS4 (Dalit Shoshit Samaj Sangharsh Samiti). However, once the BSP was formed, the element of *sangharsh*, or struggle, got conflated with the single-minded pursuit of formal power within the party competitive arena.

These instances show that given the Dalit situation and the deep resistance that caste Hindu society manifests against rightful share of Dalits in power and the public sphere, Dalit politics would always face this dilemma of whether to abandon electoral-party politics altogether or to abandon more firebrand struggles against the social order.

(The Absence of) Adivasi Politics

In India's population, the total share of the communities identified as STs is 8 per cent. However, the Adivasi population is much more concentrated in specific areas than the Dalit population. The states of North East, Odisha, Bihar (now Jharkhand), Madhya Pradesh, Maharashtra, and to some extent Chhattisgarh and Gujarat have relatively larger Adivasi population than rest of the country. However, mobilization and political organizations of the Adivasis are somewhat weak and skewed. Though not afflicted by 'untouchability' like the Dalits, Adivasis have historically suffered from relative seclusion from the caste Hindu society and its civilizational paradigm. Many Adivasi groups also had a history of armed struggles against the intruding British forces and hence a background of rebelliousness and the stamp of being 'dangerous'. At the same time, their seclusion meant that they were often not part of the politics of formal organizations that evolved during the freedom struggle and, except the communists, most parties and political groups had only very limited entry into the Adivasi societies. Though the Congress was successful in winning votes among Adivasis for a long time, the party never interested itself in mobilizing the Adivasis. The overall approach of Congress was marked by paternalism wherein devoted Congress workers would work for the 'uplift' of the Adivasis, but would not invest much energy in mobilizing the Adivasis and encouraging a culture of democratic participation. Rather than investing agency in the community itself, the emphasis was more on 'working for them'. The organizations like Admijati Sevak Sangh exemplify this tendency.

The limitation of the Congress's approach (and also that of other parties) was mainly due to the inability to understand fully the meaning of Indian nationalism and the logic of democracy vis-à-vis the Adivasi communities. Indian nationalism prevalent during the freedom struggle tended to privilege the idea of nation based on the 'mainstream' of Indian society as understood from the perspective of the Hindi heartland. Just as the Dravids were uncomfortable with that idea, many communities inhabiting the peripheries—both geographically and culturally—were not part of the national imagination beyond a vague sense of control over the land. This problem was more visible in the case of regions of the North East, but was equally relevant in the case of Adivasi communities that inhabited difficult terrains in central and western parts of the country. As a result of this blinkered imagination, the nationalist approach could not distinguish itself much from the British approach of bringing civilization to the doorsteps of the 'uncultured' Adivasis—without much respect for their traditions, their cultural mores, and, above all, their livelihoods. 'Development' in post-Independence India could not grasp the very real concerns of communities living in forests and hill areas pertaining to their livelihoods. The Congress mostly represented these limitations of the blinkered nationalist and developmentalist imaginations. These limitations did not allow the unfolding of logic of democracy in most Adivasi areas.

To complicate matters, the Rashtriya Swayamsevak Sangh (RSS) advanced a strategy to spread its voluntary work among the Adivasis with the main objective of ensuring that the Adivasis remain within the Hindu religio-cultural matrix of culture, identity, and symbolisms. The Vanvasi Kalyan Ashram worked towards neutralizing the sense of pride and self-assertion that the communist movement had instilled among the Adivasis—just as it aimed at Hinduizing the Adivasi communities—not only to wedge a distance between them and the Christian missionaries, but also to alienate them from their own traditional cultures and religious practices.

In the backdrop of the Congress and RSS approaches, the radical Marxists (Maoists) saw a potential in radicalizing the Adivasis and recruiting them to the cause of revolution. The plundering of livelihood by the developmentalist state could easily convince the Adivasis of the need to take to arms. The terrain of their inhabitations became the easy fortresses for the Maoists to engage in guerrilla warfare with the Indian state. This involvement of the Adivasis in the revolutionary cause has meant that the Indian state has got all the more reason to penetrate these regions with its military power, the net result being that both the Maoist and the statist intervention have denied agency to the Adivasis and also further postponed the exercise of democratic logic in these regions.

A similar trajectory obtains in the regions of the North East where the politics of Adivasis takes the form of demands for ethnic autonomy and separation from Indian state. The most difficult of these cases has been that of the Nagas, but even elsewhere the Adivasi communities have been mobilized for ethnic demands vis-à-vis each other (as, for instance, the demands of the Garo and Khasi communities) besides outright anti-India demands (as in the case of the ULFA in Assam). This has meant that politics in many parts of the Adivasi-majority areas of the North East manifests a duality. On the one hand, it is characterized by the militancy and assertiveness that marks insurgency and separatist demands; on the other, politics in the North East, as anywhere else, follows the routine electoral competition among local elite. In the case of the latter, the Adivasi-majority states of the North East have one other distinction. Most of these areas have parties that are specific to the state, and the presence of the so-called all-India parties like the Congress, BJP, and even for that matter the communists is very limited or almost nominal. It is possible that through this feature of localized parties, the Adivasi communities can gain a sense of agency and autonomy if they are allowed to exist and operate without being satellites of the 'national' parties.

Politics in all Adivasi areas faces perhaps the two critical challenges. One is related to the issue of balancing the pressures to 'integrate' with the larger trends prevailing in rest of the country and at the same time retain ethnic identity. The other is about safeguarding livelihoods and the prevailing ecological systems and at the same time bringing about material and infrastructural development of the regions. These are not merely challenges faced by the Adivasi communities; in true sense, these are challenges faced by democratic politics. It is not clear how democracy can sustain these contrary pressures.

Lessons from Caste Politics

The foregoing discussion does not easily yield a simplistic conclusion about the democratic experiment being able to accommodate the interests of the backward castes and communities. What then are the more durable takeaways from the inevitable entanglement of caste with competitive politics?

First, there is a somewhat tenuous link between the politics of quotas and claims made in the field of competitive politics. Politics based only on categories deriving from the constitutional–administrative framework is inadequate to address all political realities. The blocs called SCs, STs, or OBC are, after all, administrative categories mainly for the purpose of identifying the groups and giving them some common policy relief. Though oft-mentioned in the public discourse, they do not necessarily bring unity among the labelled group. In the post-Mandal era, most states have resorted to subdivision of the category of OBC into backward and more backward classes. The period after 2000 has further underscored this strategy in the light of the many agitations by castes for inclusion in the category of 'backward' classes. As Jats, Patels, Kapus, and Marathas struggle for entry in the backward category, the limits of the category called 'OBC' become evident. Even in the case of the SCs, in most states, a demand for further internal subdivision keeps recurring because of the claims of internal differentiation. This shows that there is a need to go beyond quotas in order to shape politics of social justice, but it also suggests that democratic politics itself would have to go beyond these categories.

Second, democracy makes and breaks vote banks based on caste. The complicated journey of caste politics has strengthened the criticisms that focus on caste has given rise to 'vote bank politics'. It is true that certain caste groups look upon specific leaders and/or parties as closer to their interests and hence tend to vote for them. Parties and leaders, too, treat social groups as their reliable supporters. However, as categories such as SC, ST, or OBC get challenged by internal stratifications, the idea of vote bank becomes inapplicable. We also witness the breakdown of vote-bank politics when more than one parties address the concerns of the same caste or caste group. The fragmentation of castes and caste blocs into supporters of different parties is not a very uncommon phenomenon.

The third lesson from the experience of mobilizations on caste-community basis is that such mobilizations have fractured the previous balance of social power. Democratic politics has not only delegitimized previously existing power equations based on caste hierarchy, but it has also opened the doors for new power equations to emerge.

Fourth, and perhaps the most significant, democratic politics has given rise to aspirations among 'lower castes' of exercising power. Not just a few leaders like Mulayam or Lalu Prasad, but a large number of aspirants from the backward castes now operate in the public arena more confidently than before and nurse aspirations of exercising power. The fulfilment of these aspirations is a burden for democracy, but, at least, in formal and numerical sense, a transformation has been begun, and that is an important takeaway from caste politics.

In sum, starting as an uncomfortable issue on which there were differences among the elite, by the 1990s, caste politics came to be identified as necessary for social justice and led to a consensual approach. This consensus had three by-products: (a) the search for additional pathways for achieving social justice has got indefinitely postponed; (b) the issue of poverty and material deprivation has become subsumed under the caste question; and (c) caste identities have emerged as the key foci around which mobilizations occur.

6

Towards Majoritarian Democracy

In a country full of many diversities, particularly religious diversity, the issue of relationship between majority and minority always becomes critical. More than the actual relationship between these two groups, their position in democratic polity becomes a bone of contention. What would happen if the majority community begins to claim or believe that, being a majority, it has a right to pre-eminent position in public affairs? What would happen if the majority community claims that its idea of what constitutes the nation must prevail? India's democracy has often faced these issues amid recurring tensions between the Hindu and Muslim communities. Since the 1990s, the politics around this issue has become central to democratic contestations. Developments since the elections of 2014 have further brought these issues to the centre stage. Thus, an important component of democratic politics in India consists of mobilizations and contestations around the issue of role and position of the majority community.

Partition of India took place on the insistence of the Muslim League, which claimed that Muslims constitute a separate nation. Though not all Muslims supported this demand, and though, of course, not many Muslims from the rest of India went to the newly created Pakistan (the proportion of Muslim population in India was 14.23 per cent as per the 2011 Census), the basis for that new political entity was religion. In spite of that, the Constituent Assembly of India refused to be attracted to the idea of making India a Hindu state (as a response to the idea of a Muslim Pakistan); it did not even consider that option. Instead, four cardinal principles were followed by the Constitution: that there would be no official religion of India, that no citizen shall be discriminated on grounds of religion, that every citizen shall have the right to freedom of religion, and that India would protect the cultures and languages of its minorities. These principles are consistent with the idea of democracy. These together constitute the secular state. Of course, groups which believed that Hinduism or Hindutva should constitute the basis nationalism have been active since the pre-Independence period. (The politics of Hindutva needs to be distinguished from Hindu religion. While Hindutva politics does often take position on matters of Hindu religion and invokes religious loyalties and identity to gain support, Hindutva as a political project of understanding Indian history, society, and national-ism is not the same as popular beliefs in the Hindu religious precepts and deities.)

The Context of Communalism

With Partition and the creation of Pakistan, the claims regarding Muslim 'nationalism' subsided. Nevertheless, from time to time, some Muslim groups and parties have engaged in political mobilizations based on the 'fear of the majority community' and perceptions of 'threat to Muslim religious identity'. For such groups, secularism constitutes a space to privilege religious identity over national symbols and interfaith intermin-gling. For the Hindu nationalist groups, secularism has been either a non-Indian western impostor or a merely formal constitutional framework that does not under-mine the pre-eminence of Hindu cultural nationalism.

These differences do not remain confined only to the ballot box, courtrooms, or legislative debates; they often spill over to riots and violence and put resilience of democracy to test. Such instances of violence express the deep division over what constitutes the Indian nation. The most striking example of this acerbic nature of claims over nationalism could be found in the demolition of the Babri masjid at Ayodhya in 1992. Critics of that incidence would say that it was orchestrated and systematically supported by the organizers and the state government (of Uttar Pradesh), which was sympathetic to the cause; those involved in organizing the *kar seva* (a form of religious service involving contribution to a religious cause through physical labour—an idea more prevalent among the Sikhs) would say that the large crowds that had gathered went out of control. Either way, the episode shows the fragile capacity to handle assertions of Hindu identity. That episode was preceded and followed by series of riots in many parts of India between the Hindus and Muslims. Ten years after the Babri incident, the supporters of Ram Janmabhoomi continued to undertake kar seva. In 2002, a train coach carrying *kar sevak*s, those undertaking kar seva, was put on fire at the Godhra railway station, resulting not only in the deaths of Hindu kar sevaks, but, in retaliation, the loss of hundreds of Muslim lives in a one-sided violence against Muslims across the state of Gujarat.

The politics that gave rise to the Ayodhya incidence is often referred to as communalism. The term and its application are mired in controversy. It is often employed as a criticism rather than mere description—

as something that goes against the objective of secularism. Clearly, it is not merely about organizing on the basis of a community—meaning caste, religious, or ethnic group. Communalism involves mobilization of one community vis-à-vis some other community. It believes that such mobilization is not only in the interest of the members of the community and that it is necessary to counter some other community perceived as the competitor, but it is also seen by advocates of such mobilizations as a natural ingredient of democracy. While communalism has existed right from the pre-Independence period, its salience to democratic politics remained limited in the immediate post-Independence period. From the 1990s, it became central, and the key political division came to be described as comprising the 'secular–communal' divide. Democratic politics opens up possibilities for communal polarization, but, in turn, faces a challenge from communalism.

The Hindu–Muslim divide has a long genealogy dating back to the colonial period when both communities felt threatened by each other's claims. When the colonial government began contemplating participation by the Indians in government and administration, the two communities began making claims about share in power on the basis of religion. This competition for greater share in power gradually evolved into ideological claims to being national communities. While some

Muslim leaders refused to accept that a multireligious Indian society could become a nation, some Hindu leaders insisted that common religion is an important basis for becoming a nation, and, in the Indian context, Hindu religion (and Hindu culture) could alone be the basis for national awakening and identity. In the third and fourth decades of the twentieth century, Muslim claims translated into demands for separate national political arrangement for the Muslims (Pakistan). In post-Partition period, the Muslim separatist claims became weak or non-existent, but the claims of a separate Muslim identity and the need for a separate treatment of 'minorities' continued to be expressed and also continued to attract opposition. The claims of Hindu nationalism, on the other hand, continued to nurse the ambition of becoming acceptable to the majority of the Hindu community, and, thus, the politics of Hindu mobilization became an important aspect of competitive politics in India.

Journey of Hindu Nationalism

There are many shades to the Hindu nationalist argument, and historically at least two distinct variants have existed: articulated by Savarkar and Golwalkar. Savarkar was influenced by the Italian nationalist tradition, which was not necessarily averse to formal democracy, but nonetheless believed in the necessity of complete unity stemming from uniformity in matters of culture, historical memory, and possibly language and religion. Savarkar was influenced by social Darwinism and the Indian tradition of upholding violence for a good cause as religious duty. However, both his rationalism and his search for national power drove Savarkar to a reformist position in matters of social and religious reform, and his rationalism also prompted him to shun rituals and vacuous worship. This made him less acceptable to the Hindu nationalists who believed in the orthodox prac-tices of Hinduism as essential and sacred. Golwalkar represented this genre of Hindu nationalism, and hence there was a tense distance between the two variants of Hindu nationalism, respectively, led by the RSS under Golwalkar and Hindu Mahasabha under Savarkar. But both variants agreed that Hindu religious past, Hindu culture, and Hindu-ness must constitute the basis of Indian nationalism. Both also agreed on the unsuitability of Muslims to this nationalist project, and were vehement in their deep philosophical and equally strong political opposition to Gandhi and the Congress. Thus, even during the pre-Independence period, the division was clear—between the Hindu nationalists, and the Congress and other political groups. The latter believed that nationalism can be an emancipatory project—that it did not have to be based on religion, religio-cultural aspects, or language and ethnicity. In fact, the non-Hindutva nationalist project was keen to accommodate all diversities and yet fulfil the nationalist ambition of oneness and common purpose. In this group, too, there were internal variations as those between Gandhians, modernists led by Nehru, anti-caste and anti-Congress leaders like Ambedkar, and the communists, who believed that India was not one nation, but a conglomerate of nationalities. But they all had one thing in common: they disagreed fundamentally with the premises of Hindu nationalists about religion as the basis of nationalism and about Hindu-ness being the essence of Indian nationalism.

So, it is necessary to remember that the core contestation centred on the question of what the role of Hindu-ness (either understood as being the traits of the Hindu religion or cultural traits based in Hindu social history) would be in constructing and sustaining the Indian nation. As a corollary, this core difference also brought in sharp focus the issue of dealing with non-Hindu communities. The Hindu nationalists would argue that non-Hindu communities needed to adopt a Hindu cultural way and lifestyle in order to gel with Indian nationalism, and if they did not, their loyalty to Indian nationalism would remain suspect (and for many a Hindu nationalists, the non-Hindus have always remained suspects in any case). By contrast, the non-Hindutva nationalist thinking would believe that India's nationalism was capable of accommodating all religious groups and that faith did not define one's national identity. They also believed that non-Hindu communities constituted a minority, and as such, in a democratic set up, these communities deserved some state protection to advance their culture because democracy and Indian nationalism did not preclude them from retaining their separate religious identity within the new national political community called Indian nation state. In fact, the strong majority that Hindu community was set to enjoy in India prompted many nationalists to believe that minority rights were necessary as a political arrangement in independent India.

While the non-Hindutva variant of nationalism would always emphasize that democracy meant accommodation of all religious communities and, therefore, democracy and nationalism would be compatible only if the interests of the minorities were protected, Hindu nationalists have often wondered why there should be any tension between democracy and predominance of the sentiments of the 'majority' community. They find it odd that in the name of democracy, the aspirations and identity of the majority community should be set aside or downplayed. Thus, in this debate over national identity, the issue of competing meanings of democracy is inextricably involved.

In the pre-Independence period, Congress under Gandhi and Nehru was successful in occupying the nationalist space. The Hindu nationalists mostly remained a fringe or a mute element during that phase. The masses mostly followed the Congress leadership both in the course of the freedom struggle and in the limited electoral politics that took place under British rule. This peripheral position of the Hindu nationalists was also reflected in the composition of the Constituent Assembly and its overall thinking. Nonetheless, it must be remembered that while organizationally the Hindu nationalists were not a strong force in the making of the Constitution, within the Congress there were many voices which echoed the Hindu nationalist thinking and a desire to make new India culturally more Hindu. In other words, the Congress politically dominated the Hindu nationalist organizations, but that did not preclude the Congress from having within its fold leaders and groups with sympathies for various aspects of the Hindu nationalist project.

Nehru's popularity with the masses and his attempts to shift the political debates after Independence to issues of welfare could successfully keep the Hindu nationalist politics confined to limited social sections. Savarkar never could pose a political threat in post-Independence electoral arena. The main political competition to Congress's pluralist national imagination came from the RSS and the Bharatiya Jan Sangh. While the RSS remained undaunted in its pursuit of orthodox and ritualistic Hindutva, as a political party, the Jan Sangh attempted to broad-base its politics while remaining ideologically rooted in Hindu nationalism. But its ideological appeal could only attract sections of the upper caste–middle class voters. In states where the Jan Sangh collaborated with the sections of princely rulers and the Swatantra Party, it could register relatively impressive electoral performance. But otherwise, Jan Sangh continued to be a minor political force until the politics of coalitions opposed to Indira Gandhi's Congress began to shape since the late 1960s. Its vote share was in the range of 6 per cent in 1957 and 1962 parliamentary elections, which rose to over 9 per cent in 1967 during the coalition era, but fell to 7.4 per cent during the height of Indira wave of 1971.

The Bharatiya Janata Party

It is in this context that the rise of BJP needs to be taken into account. Formed in 1980, the BJP explicitly adheres to Hindu nationalism and claims to be the continuation of the erstwhile Jana Sangh. The BJP began with a rather lacklustre performance in 1984, but that election had a rather extraordinary context of assassination of Indira Gandhi. From 11.5 per cent votes in 1989, the party went on to poll 20 per cent votes in 1991 and reached almost 26 per cent in 1998. The electoral ascendance of the BJP in the period after 1989 is a complex phenomenon since it combines appeal of Hindu nationalism and the changes occurring in the party political arena. In this phase, the decline of the Congress was indeed helpful in propelling the BJP into electoral prominence. Within 10 years from emerging as a major player in 1989, the BJP had become the main architect of the ruling coalition in 1998, and finally in 2014, it won a clear majority in Lok Sabha and polled its highest ever vote share till then—31 per cent. It is not easy to surmise that all BJP voters actively support Hindu nationalism; nevertheless, the minimum that we can surmise is that for almost one-third of the voters, Hindu nationalism did not pose a problem strong enough not to vote for the BJP.

In 2014, the BJP's campaign successfully combined the idea of nationalism with the idea of development. After coming to power, the BJP continued to pursue the ideological offensive. The conflation of the three factors—development, nationalism, and Hindutva—resulted in sustained support for the party after the parliamentary election. Apart from propelling the party into the position of a central political force, this conflation shaped a broader base for the idea of Hindu nationalism and made that ideology electorally viable for the first time since Independence. But more than the potential to win elections, these developments since 2014 indicate that the overall acceptance of the Hindutva ideology is gaining ground, and the public sphere is slowly moving towards a Hindu nationalist perspective.

What happened outside the electoral arena between the 1970s and the first decade of the twentieth century, however, merits attention in terms of the key contestation mentioned earlier. In the 1970s, the RSS under the leadership of Deoras began to shift its ideological focus and political strategy. While the core belief in Hindu nationalism remained constant, the meaning of Hindu nationalism shifted to the Savarkarite position discussed earlier—it began to put less emphasis on orthodoxy and traditional caste–varna system and more on militant, anti-Muslim rhetoric uniting all Hindus, and it also began to spread its work among the Adivasis and later among the Dalits. These moves allowed the BJP to claim that it indeed represented 'Hindu' interests and also made it possible for the party to build a broad-based social coalition of multiple sections of the Hindu community. More specifically, this move allowed the BJP to popularize its Hindu nationalism among cross-sections of the Hindu society instead of the somewhat narrow popularity of the Hindutva agenda only among the upper castes.

Also, the issue that the BJP and RSS raised from the mid-1980s caught the imagination of ordinary Hindus irrespective of caste and class—the issue of Ram Janmabhoomi at Ayodhya. Reams have been written on the history, legality, archaeology, and mythology attached to the Ayodhya site to support or refute the claims of the Hindu nationalists. However, two things need to be noted: first, that the RSS was successful in creating some sympathy among the majority of Hindus on the Ayodhya question; for many Hindus, this became an issue of justice, pride, and nationalism. Second, and following from the first, while the opponents of RSS–BJP got involved in lengthy intellectual battles over ideology and history concerning the site at Ayodhya, for the BJP, not the construction of the temple but political mobilization and shaping of a certain nationalist thinking were the key issues. The Ayodhya issue surfaced during the mid-1980s and gathered momentum during the somewhat inexperienced and politically less tactical leadership of Rajiv Gandhi. The high point of the agitation was the Rath Yatra led by Advani that ensured a full-fledged communal mobilization in favour of the BJP across many parts of the country.

The destruction of the disputed mosque by mobs of Hindu nationalists in 1992 symbolically expressed the non-democratic possibilities involved in the Hindu mobilizations. The events of December 1992 thus represent not only institutional failure, but also the weakness of democratic practice. The year 1992—like 1975, discussed in the second chapter—represents the deep-rooted weakness of democracy. If 1975 manifested the institutional weakness more, 1992 manifested the weakness of practice. But weakness of practice is often predicated on institutional weakness—the inability of the police to protect citizens impartially is one part of that weakness; the inability of the political executive to take quick and effective action forms the political side of that weakness. But above all, two factors constitute the core narrative: that the democratic system does not have enough political disincentives for such mob violence and that legitimation of mob violence is possible.

The anti-Muslim violence of 2002 in Gujarat took this narrative further. Many critics of the Congress draw attention to the anti-Sikh riots of 1984, in which many Congress leaders were allegedly implicated, as something similar to the anti-Muslim violence of 2002. While this comparison is possible, a crucial difference needs to be noted. For the BJP and Hindu nationalists, the idea of nation is based on the exclusion of one community, and this exclusionary idea informs their electoral politics as well as popular mobilizations. Therefore, the BJP has neither shown remorse over the destruction of the Babri masjid nor apologized over the massacre of Muslims in Gujarat in 2002. (It was in power in the two states at those specific moments.) And the worrying point is that both these incidents had no adverse effect whatsoever on the BJP's electoral prospects. In 1996, its vote share remained stable—in fact marginally improved over 1991, and in 2004, though the party lost power, it lost only 1.6 per cent votes compared to 1999. And, of course, following the 2002 violence, it won the Gujarat state elections even more handsomely than before, increasing its vote share by 5 per cent—from 44.8 per cent in 1998 to 49.8 per cent. So, the obvious lesson is that even by riding on an anti-democratic wave of mob violence, parties and leaders can still enjoy electoral victories with impunity.

What Happened to 'Muslim Politics'?

Since the Muslim League was identified with Partition, it could not have political acceptability in post-Independence India. This situation meant that the large Muslim community that chose to remain in India after Partition did not have any political vehicle specifically attending to its needs and aspirations. The Congress party mostly sought to fill this void—both because of ideological reasons that it believed in a national political community comprising of all religious groups and because of the political calculations that, with Muslim support, the party would be more inclusive and more politically invincible. But the Congress's inclusiveness and its perception of the minority complex among the Muslims meant that the Congress could not support social reform among the Muslims nor could it persuade them to adopt a non-communal approach to politics. Instead, the party kept vacillating between what its critics called appeasement of the Muslims and a neglect of the key material interests of the Muslim community. Large sections of the Muslims thus remained under the influence of Muslim clergy, who also doubled up as their political leaders. In West Bengal, the Muslims did get attracted to the communists, but elsewhere, including Bihar and Uttar Pradesh, the community was more influenced by the Congress than any other parties. This political situation lent some credence to the criticisms that Muslims were the 'vote bank' of the Congress party. This picture however began to change in the post-1975 period when the Muslims in many parts of the country began to explore non-Congress alternatives such as the Janata Party in 1977, the JD in 1989, and various breakaway factions of the JD in the post-1990 period. In Uttar Pradesh, Mulayam Singh's politics came to be based on Muslim support, while in Bihar parties led by Lalu Prasad and Nitish Kumar received consistently more support from the Muslims. In West Bengal, the Left front was popular among the Muslims for the major part since the 1970s, but after the decline of the Left front since 2011, the Muslim community chose the Trinamool Congress as its main political instrument. Along with the state-based parties winning support from the Muslim community, there are also instances of new parties exclusively catering to the aspirations of Muslims having emerged in some states. The All India United Democratic Front led by Badruddin Ajmal in Assam and All India Majlis-e-Ittehadul Muslimeen led by the Owaisis are cases in point. At a superficial level, this might look like 'politics of vote bank'. However, the continued existence of politics of Hindutva has meant that the Muslims, who are depicted as suspect and less loyal to Indian nation, would tend to search for a political vehicle that would protect their interests. This situation leads to a dilemma: in a democracy, political parties need not be and should not be based on communities, but politics of Hindutva not only exhorts the Hindus to unite politically, it also forces the other communities, particularly the Muslims, to behave as one bloc. Existence of Hindutva politics produces its mirror image among the Muslim community in the form of parties, leaders, and groups that would often take a community-based stand on public matters. It is in this sense that the term 'communalism' is employed to denote both Hindu and Muslim (or for that matter any other religion-based) politics.

While both Hindu and Muslim communities have political groups that tend to mobilize on the basis of religious identity, there is a critical difference. Hindu mobilization is based on a certain construction of Indian nationalism, whereas the post-Independence Muslim mobilization, though on the basis of religion, does not invoke a Muslim national imagination. The propagation of Hindu nationalism is thus a distinguishing feature of Hindu communal mobilization and has at least three deeper implications for democratic politics.

Competitive Communalism

Competitive communalism refers to demands and mobilizations that pertain to group identity, labels, symbols, histories, memories, sense of hurt, sense of pride, and so on, more than life conditions. Thus, communalism subsumes issues of life conditions within the larger narrative of symbols, identities, and perceptions. As noted, Hindu–Muslim relations have had a history of not only conflicts, but continued competition. This often leads to competitive communalism—each community begins thinking of itself in terms of community-based symbols, demands, identities, and mobilizations, so that it has a competitive advantage in the democratic numbers game. The public debates are often structured in the format of 'If they do it why not us....' Demands or actions are not judged by whether they are right or wrong, but by a certain reciprocity. If a 'concession' is allegedly accorded to one community, it is balanced by another concession to the other—competing—community. (In this regard, it is interesting to note that Prime Minister Modi chose to adopt this same approach while campaigning in Uttar Pradesh assembly election in 2017 when he told his audience that equal treatment of communities means that if there is power supply on Eid, then same must happen in case of Diwali also; see *Indian Express* 2017.) Politics then becomes a delicate balance of community concessions and identities, and democracy is understood as democracy of communities rather than democracy of persons or interests. (This feature is also augmented by the politics of caste.)

The Hindu–Muslim polemic in particular is always structured through this logic of community balance rather than fairness and justice. Hindutva politics demands that 'Hindu' concerns be recognized as concerns of the majority, while the politicians mobilizing the Muslims make claims on the basis of a 'minority' status. For the Hindus, as will be seen ahead, their numeric majority is sufficient argument for the democratic nature of their claims, and for the Muslims, their minority status and its protection is the litmus test of democracy. Ironically, while the two conceptions of democracy do not easily get reconciled, they indeed produce tension both between communities and between meanings of democracy.

This situation also leads to a genuine theoretical dilemma. Is there something wrong if religious or ethnic communities organize politically without recognizing internal differences—that is, is community affiliation a condition enough to claim a common interest, or should democratic politics encourage intermixing of communities and overlapping of community identities for purposes of forming political interests? Politics of communalism tends to privilege community identity over other sociopolitical interests, and, in the process, also creates homogenous and essentializing categories as Hindus, Muslims, Christians, or majorities and minorities. This is problematic since such identity formation endangers possible individuality of persons and groups within a given community.

Competitive Hindutva?

During the period when Babri masjid was destroyed, a phrase had gained currency among the critics of Hindutva politics—'soft Hindutva'. It was argued that the Congress under Narsimha Rao was adopting a soft Hindutva line. For the 'hard' secularists, any concession not only to the BJP–RSS, but to the Hindu sentiment was morally wrong. But parties are in the business of power and competition. This compulsion necessarily moves them into the proximity of public opinion and prejudice (unless they have the capacity to move public opinion away from prejudice). As the BJP gained popularity for its Hindutva rhetoric, other parties were bound to be tempted to adopt a position acceptable to the Hindutva constituency. At least there would be disincentives to criticize and oppose Hindutva strongly.

Narasimha Rao's prevarication over the question of taking a stand against Hindutva was not the first instance of such ambivalences. The harsh nationalist rhetoric unleashed by Indira Gandhi during first half of the 1980s, in response to the Khalistan issue, could easily become indistinguishable from some precepts of Hindu nationalism. As already hinted earlier, the anti-Sikh violence in the aftermath of her assassination had all the elements of a nationalist fury of the mob—a sentiment that was directed against the 'enemy within'.

The structure of that politics of violence was not different from the structure of the Hindu national-ist argument—that there is a danger from within the society to the national cause, and a tough action by the government, and if not by the government then by the nation–loving masses, can alone purge or limit that danger. As Savarkarites would put it, violence for the just cause of nation is no violence; it is sacrifice and duty. It is another matter whether the mobs engaging in street violence either in the case of the anti–Sikh violence or in the case of the anti–Muslim violence later in Gujarat would be steeped in this philosophical justification of violence, but they could be aroused in the name of nation and against an internal 'enemy', and, subsequently, their violent actions could be explained/ justified on the basis of nationalism and 'violence as religious duty' argument. So, the ingredients of Hindu nationalism were already being cultivated and accepted into the political process since the mid–1980s.

As the BJP and its Hindu nationalist rhetoric began gaining momentum, political parties must have won-dered if they would lose votes—naturally mostly the Hindu votes—unless they also obliquely acquiesced in some aspects of Hindu symbolisms and ideas of Hindu nationalism. During the 1990s, parties like the SP and RJD, that had a different agenda and a firm social constituency behind them, could afford to take on the Hindu nationalism of the BJP, but Congress, which was already in decline mode, could hardly afford to do that. So, the Congress party shrank from an ideological battle with the BJP and consequently ceded ground. In Tamil Nadu, the tough bipolarity of the politics of the state pushed the AIADMK towards an indirect Hindutva line in its practice if not in precept. During the mid-1980s, the Shiv Sena in Maharashtra, too, adopted an explicitly pro-Hindutva position when it decided to expand beyond the Mumbai–Thane belt. The larger issue then is this: would eventually many more parties succumb to this electoral lure of Hindutva and adopt the strategy of wooing Hindu votes through celebrating Hindu symbols, Hindu icons, and thereby strengthening the politics of Hindu nationalism?

The division between the politics of Hindutva and politics opposed to Hindu communalism has remained central since the mid-1980s. But that is no guarantee that it would always remain so. Electoral compulsions forced many parties to ally with the BJP in spite of both Ayodhya controversy and later in the backdrop of the anti-Muslim violence in Gujarat. The argument of those parties was that they did not subscribe to the BJP's Hindu nationalism, but aligned with it mainly to throw away their main enemy—the Congress. From this pragmatic political calculation, it is only one step for them to argue that accommodating some elements of Hindutva and conceding to some demands of the Hindus is politically expedient in the competitive context.

While many parties and their leaders have consistently desisted from approving the core arguments of Hindu nationalism, in a country with a huge Hindu majority and with a long history of mobilization of Hindus on the basis of Hindu identity and symbols, it is difficult for most parties and leaders not to invoke Hindu cultural practices and symbols.

Majoritarianism

Therefore, the most critical effect that the politics of communalism in general and Hindutva politics in particular has produced may be described as the strengthening of majoritarian tendency. Structurally, electoral democracy based on simple majority is always susceptible to a majoritarian understanding of what democracy constitutes. This possibility becomes even more pronounced when the social context is comprised of a majority community and many minority groups. In such situations, the majority group begins to understand democracy in terms of its fixed/assured majority. While, procedurally, democracy would mean rule by the majority as established through elections, majoritarian understanding of democracy would expect that social/ethnic majorities would always also constitute political majority. In a sense, the Muslim League's logic behind finally claiming certain territories from British India to become Pakistan was informed by this majoritarian logic. The League believed that because the Hindus were a majority, the Muslims would not get just treatment in it politically and, therefore, 'Muslim-majority' areas should constitute a separate political entity because religious majority constitutes the basis for formation of political community.

In post-Independence India, various Hindu organizations always propagated this majoritarian view of democracy. They would argue that because Hindus are a majority in India, it is only natural that national identity and social–cultural norms in India have to be based on Hindutva. This belief stems from what we have referred to as democracy of communities rather than democracy of citizens. All democratic societies with diversity would face this complex issue. It would be artificial to expect that citizens would entirely give up or set aside their various sociocultural identities. Hence, in a democracy, citizens would always bring in their identities as bases for claims and even for organization. Yet, theoretically, democracy would expect citizens to rise above all such identities and adopt the civic virtue—that by adopting overlapping identities, citizens should privilege civic rationality and public interest over group identities and sectional interests. In other words, democracy expects a competitive and yet balanced relationship between group or community identities and individuality as the competing bases for comprehending public interest. But in reality, many societies experience an ascendance of group identities over everything else.

Politics of Hindutva has tapped the majoritarian tendencies among the Hindus and constructed a narrative of how the Hindus are not getting their just due in a Hindu majority India. The huge organizational efforts and the long years of systematic propaganda began to bear fruit during the political vacuum created by the decline of the Congress and the failure of the JD (and its factions) around 1990. On the communal question, this majoritarian understanding of democracy has yet not fully established itself. But, as this author has argued, since 2004, the Hindutva rhetoric and BJP's political successes have produced a critical body of support for the majoritarian viewpoint, and increasingly the core political battle has shifted to issues of the normative middle ground of politics. While there is not enough evidence to argue that the BJP won the 2014 elections only because of this majoritarianism, what is in fact more important is that there is some evidence to suggest that majoritarian voters are spread across parties—giving credence to the argument that majoritarian norms are indeed becoming the middle ground of Indian politics.

The majoritarian tendency leads to an imagination that democracy means rule by group/s that constitute majority in the social-ethnic sense. This same logic often informs the politics of regional claims. A community claims certain rights because it constitutes majority in a given region. Hindu nationalism ideologically feeds on, and in turn strengthens, this majoritarian understanding of democracy. But majoritarianism is by no means restricted to only Hindu nationalism. For instance, there was disappointment among the Sikhs of Punjab that even after carving out Haryana (and ensuring a Sikh majority state), the AD could not control power in the state. Similarly, the understanding of Naga identity vis-à-vis the Manipuris or vice versa is based on a majoritarian perspective—just as the demands from groups within Meghalaya or Assam often combine economic and developmental issues with issues of localized majoritarian aspirations and construction of 'outsiders'.

These overlapping and intertwined effects of the politics of Hindutva (and, of course, politics of Muslim communalism as well) produce two key distortions in democratic politics. First, these features obstruct the shaping of a public reason and culture of deliberations.

Instead, mutual suspicion and search for an enemy within the society become a common strategy adopted by each community. The balance between community and the imaginary democratic citizen is lost in such situations. Democracy does not become an arena of mutual respect and negotiation, but gets reduced to mutual blackmail and therefore inability to reach compromises. The Ayodhya dispute is a classic instance of this. In the backdrop of the destruction of the mosque and subsequent violence, any compromise would appear only as surrender for the Muslim community. So, the democratic hope of negotiated settlement is permanently lost. Moreover, division of society into permanent barricades becomes an insurance against the shaping of a robust idea of collective well-being and common good.

Second, and relatedly, majoritarianism and its 'other'—minorityism—intervenes in the valuable heritage of diversity. Diversity is seen from the prism of the majority–minority frame, or diversity is entirely ignored. The diversity of languages, cultural practices, religious ideas, faiths, and traditions tend to lose its innate value. These diversities get divided between identity marks of particular communities to differentiate them from each other. The value of diversity is in its capacity to enrich through interaction and exchange, but majoritarianism transforms diversity into markers of difference that cannot be trespassed and into sign-posts of community boundaries.

It is this double loss—the loss of public-ness and loss of diversity—that is the likely effect of the increasingly strengthening trend of majoritarianism, in the process, shrinking the democratic space in both politics and social relations.

7

Paradoxes, Diversions, and Distortions

Democracy seldom has a seamless journey—it is full of multiple possibilities. Democracy brings out excitements and passions that may lead in different directions. India's democracy is no exception. In fact, the historical setting in which democracy first emerged in India and the many contextual problems that it faced have made Indian democracy a somewhat inconsistent phenomenon. It is inconsistent in the sense that groups and individuals steadfastly upholding democracy in one context or situation extend only weak support to it in some other situation; people express their full support to democracy and yet settle for sub-democratic options. Thus, citizen support to democracy has contextual variation. Indian democracy is inconsistent also in the sense that different arenas of life manifest varying degrees of democracy. This variation means that individual dignity and group claims receive popular support in some arenas of public life, but they may be less acceptable in some other arenas. Thus, political equality is upheld in the arena of party politics and electoral competition, but not so much in the field of governance. Similarly, claims of caste groups are recognized as important and valid, but claims of minority religious communities are always suspect. This same inconsistency is witnessed in the behaviour of democratic institutions in India.

Because of such inconsistencies, it is quite easy a task to find fault with India's democracy. If one were to list the 'problems' faced by India's democracy, they would be practically countless! From social inequality to slow pace of development to electoral malpractices to elite takeover to so many other problems. But then, which democracy does not have problems? So, pointing at Indian democracy's problems does not tell us much—it only underscores the fact that like all other democracies, India's democracy also exists in an imperfect environment and the democratic project, like anywhere else, is a 'work in progress'.

But if one were to specifically develop a framework of evaluation for India's democracy and wanted to map its journey, where does one look? Given its inconsistent nature, the ambivalences ingrained in this enterprise, and the multifaceted characteristics it has

154

developed, rather than pronouncing a 'balance sheet' of India's democracy, it is useful to locate the key paradoxes that mark the functioning of India's democracy. Similarly, the journey of India's democracy—through these paradoxes and *because* of them—is full of diversions and possibilities of distortions. Grasping these paradoxes, diversions, and distortions helps us become better judges of, and better participants in, this enterprise called Indian democracy.

Paradox One

Quite often, democracy is identified with elections. For most citizens, elections constitute the only window through which they can jump into the courtyards of power, momentarily. The electoral arena has many accomplishments to its credit as far as Indian democracy is concerned. Not only do Indian people approve of electoral democracy overwhelmingly, they also believe that their vote matters. (In 2013, two persons out of every three believed that their vote made a difference.) Over time, the belief in elections has also increased because people tend to think that electoral malpractices have become less and less. (In 2013, 6 per cent said that there were many problems in the way elections are conducted, and another 7 per cent felt elections were not fair.) People's participation in elections has also reached a robust level comparable to most democracies. As already noted, turnout in national elections often touches 60 per cent and is much more than that in most state assembly elections. Reported participation in campaigns is also quite high (17 per cent), and about 38 per cent people identify themselves as 'close to some party or the other' (Lokniti 2015; SDSA Team 2008).

This vibrancy of electoral arena, however, gets punctured when one begins to look at the underbelly of electoral politics. Electoral politics is infamous for the huge financial resources that it demands. This makes it next to impossible for ordinary citizens to think of active participation in elections beyond campaign participation. Moreover, the collection of money (and its spending) remain shrouded in mystery. There are no restrictions on how much a party should spend on elections. Existing rules require a candidate to submit the accounts of money spent on elections, but everyone suspects that mythical amounts are spent, often in dubious manner. Organizations like the Association for Democratic Reforms have been publicizing this aspect of elections in India and have been pushing for substantial electoral reforms (Association for Democratic Reforms).

Thus, the source of money that is spent and the manner in which it is spent are two key problems in electoral politics. Beyond promises and policies to obtain loyalty of sections of voters, there are allegations of 'vote buying' either through distribution of consumer goods, benefits, etc., among the electorate or more crass distribution of money among voters. In any case, the near-obscene use of money during elections downgrades the democratic character of elections. Also, the local electoral context is often too murky to match the idealized picture of elections that we imagine. This murkiness is not just because of conspiracies and intrigues, it is more because of the crass muscle power that is involved. While electoral violence has certainly come down after the 1990s, there are places, localities, villages, and even states where 'sensitive' situation occurs during campaign and voting.

So, here is the paradox. Elections have a central place in democratic practice in India; elections also have considerable legitimacy and large-scale social acceptance, but the underside of elections makes them very unattractive and raises questions about the democratic authenticity of the exercise.

Paradox Two

India has a strong democratic framework—its Constitution is founded on robust democratic thinking, and its civil and military bureaucracies are trained and expected to function within broader democratic framework under the political masters. The institutional arrangement is supposed to protect individual liberties and also balance the diverse sectional interests in society through negotiation and compromise. More importantly, the Constitution seeks to address the issue of empowering the state and, at the same time, ensures a humane and democratic state. This is indeed a tall order because, by nature, the state is inclined to restrict freedoms, resort to regulative powers, and become a repository of repressive urges that prevail in society. Democracy is an ongoing struggle to tame the state, make it amenable to reason, and reduce its craving for regulation and repression. The efforts in this direction are quite evident in the Constitution. But the Indian state, over the past seven decades, has often defied the democratic logic and underscored its repressive stateness at the cost of freedoms. The undemocratic and repressive recesses in India's institutional practices are sometimes not only worrying, but also fearsome. This defiance of the Constitutional spirit of democracy takes two forms. One emanates from state practices adopted by bureaucracy, police, armed forces, and others. These institutions often behave in an anti-people manner. Thus, one keeps hearing of 'excesses' and 'encounters' besides plain misbehaviour and unlawful actions.

But perhaps more seriously, the formal choices of the state, in terms of laws and regulations, often transgress the democratic spirit. From preventive detentions to anti-terror laws to use of anti-sedition law to laws pertaining to organized crime to special powers accorded to police, paramilitary, or armed forces in 'disturbed' areas—the paraphernalia of repressive legislation has kept expanding and receiving judicial approval in most cases. The thin line between security and law and order, on the one hand, and trigger-happy repressive instincts of the state apparatus, on the other, is always deceptively blurred.

Thus, we often come across the second paradox: India has a long history of struggle against colonial state which sought to restrict the realm of individual liberties; it has a robust democratic culture of popular mobilization and assertion, and a constitutional document that flows from the democratic logic of limited government. And yet, experience of the last seven decades shows that the state has acquired many undemocratic powers, and its practice too routinely smacks of contempt for people and their rights.

Paradox Three

Right from the nineteenth century, many political mobilizations have often hinged on 'identities'.

Therefore, the questions of relationship between identity and interest, on the one hand, and identity politics and democracy, on the other, have always been critical to the nature of democratic politics in India. It would be a mistake to imagine that citizens develop only abstract, individuated personalities completely devoid of any affection or engagement with community ties. Language, region, religion, caste, ethnicity, etc., are all very likely candidates for individuals' affections. Democratic contestations are as much about such identities as they are about material concerns or life conditions. So, democracies would always witness, allow, and even facilitate popular mobilizations on the basis of identities. Besides, 'identities' are often entangled with material locations of groups. Caste is not just a question of identity; it is much more a question of life chances and inequalities involving differences in social status and economic well-being. This is equally true of minority religious communities or Adivasi communities. Thus, while we can conceptually separate identity from material condition, social reality produces a combination of the two, and this makes politics of identity even more commonplace in democracies. In India, therefore, we often witness community mobilizations that exhibit the flag of common identity, but are primarily concerned with issues of survival and/or dignity.

The period of demands for statehood was a phase of explosion of language/region-based identities. After 1978, the explosion of caste identities took place and, subsequently, we have also been witnessing explosion of religious identities. Each one of these facilitated the articulation of anxieties and concerns of sections that otherwise might have been consigned to the larger category called 'people'. The focus on identity, however, ensured their differentiation from other groups and also meant an emphasis on group-specific issues of recognition, accommodation, and well-being.

At the same time, this style of mobilization also meant that interests and publicness could be comprehended only through the prism of identity. In each of these phases, we come across arguments that tend to mix the material with the symbolic. But in the post-1990 period, the material aspects of community concerns slowly became less salient compared to the emotive and symbolic concerns. The post-1990 phase may in fact be described as the *identity turn* in India's democratic politics. This 'turn' included two contrasting identity mobilizations. On the one hand, it included mobilizations based on wider, homogenizing identities or mega-identities such as 'OBC', Muslim, and Hindu identity mobilizations; on the other, a wide range of more specific and fragmented identities also emerged during this phase. In India's North East, this took the form of rise of tribe-specific identity mobilization, while in other parts, the form of caste-specific mobilizations. But whether homogenizing or fragmenting, identity politics—and an overemphasis on it—raise several complex issues.

One issue is about the relationship between identity and representation. Legislatures, executives, party bodies, and so on, need to reflect the multiplicity of identity-based aspirations, and yet a merely mechanical reflection of every community does not necessarily ensure true representation of the community or its interests. In other words, it is a moot question if mirror images of society truly ensure representation of all 'parts' and also representation of the 'whole'. Another complex issue is the gradual decoupling of identity from interest. As noted earlier, excessive concern with identity leads to a search for tokens, symbols, heroes, and spokespersons rather than systematic pursuance of community's interests. This might lead to a situation where politics is conducted in the language of identity and yet interest of members of groups are not necessarily cared for. Moreover, as identities become frozen, every identity group tends to believe in the exclusive authenticity of its own demands and expectations. As a result, the space for negotiation shrinks and democracy becomes impossible to function. Whether in the case of demands by various castes for inclusion in a particular category (Gujjars demanding inclusion in ST category, Patels or Marathas demanding inclusion in OBC category, and so on), or in the case of regions/states (Karnataka versus Tamil Nadu on the Cauvery issue or Punjab, Haryana, and Rajasthan on Sutlej waters), one witnesses this near deadlock of democratic negotiation as a result of identity excess.

So, the third paradox is as follows: India's democratic politics has become richer and more representative because of identity mobilizations, but identity mobilizations have also produced erosion of democratic spirit of negotiation and accommodation as democracy takes the form of assortment of autonomous, identity-based republics.

Paradox Four

Diversity is the most celebrated feature of Indian society. The creation of national sentiment within the context of this diversity has been a fascinating process. After Independence, conscious efforts were made both constitutionally and in political practice to live happily with this diversity. It is of course not the case that India is so unique that no other nation state has much diversity, but there are two aspects of India's diversity that still require attention. On the one hand, India's diversity is by far the most complex and overlapping social phenomenon, and besides scale and size, what distinguishes India is the overlapping pattern of diversity. For instance, just as there is 'religious' diversity between Hindus and Muslims, there is linguistic diversity among both these communities. So, it is not easy to privilege any one basis of diversity over all others. Secondly, in the post-Independence period, the overall emphasis has been to let these diverse social groups retain their separate cultural existences. This has given certain sanctity to the idea of diversity—so much so that India's nationalism and India's democratic practice cannot be imagined without their varied diversities. Diversity, thus, is not merely a social given, an empirical fact willy-nilly accepted; it is a foundational principle of both nationalism and democracy in India. To put it provocatively, no community has to give up its identity in order to be, or to 'prove' being, Indian.

While it is expected that democracy and nationalism would thus privilege diversity, both also intervene in the process of shaping the fate of diverse groups and the fate of intergroup relations. Nationalism puts a premium on homogeneity, and though nationalism in India seeks to respect diversity, a natural side effect of nationalist rhetoric always produces unease as far as diversities are concerned. Democracy has a more complex impact on diversity. It facilitates and even encourages the assertion of separate identity of various diverse social groupings. At the same time, the democratic requirement of constructing a larger public leads to homogenization. By nature, parties seek to build not only instrumental political coalitions, they also contribute to the building of cross-sectional groups that acquire homogenized identities. Electoral democracy, in particular, is famous for this contradictory relationship with diversity. Parties based on ethnic appeal do have space in electoral politics (particularly when politics become more competitive), but such parties then get imprisoned by their following and hence cannot grow beyond those communities. This encourages parties and competitive politics to evolve common platforms, common vocabularies, common imageries, and even common vices, gradually undercutting the diversity of existences. While a typical complaint about 'politics' is often that it fragments, that it sharpens differences, that it juxtaposes one community against the other, politics in reality produces an amazing amount of homogenization of ideas and practices, penetrating the cultural defences of most communities.

This brings us to the fourth and a deeper paradox: the urge for underscoring separate existence and the push towards homogenization constitute the cusp at which India's diversities exist today. One would hope democracy to strengthen diversities and also make them not only coexist, but also prepare them to negotiate and compromise. However, democracy also tends to obliterate diversities and fundamentally change the meaning of diversity. So, the paradox is that India's democracy is expected to be the protector of diversities, but its practice has often tended to strengthen forces of homogenization.

Paradox Five

When India embarked on the journey of formal democracy, it was predominantly poor. The economic backwardness of the country was not just confined to macroeconomic parameters of the gross domestic product and the like—as a country, India was of course poor, but a very large section of its population also was very poor. Debates in Indian economics have been marked by the differences among experts on what constitutes poverty and how to calculate the numbers of the poor in the country's population. But the fact of a large population being poor, living in subhuman conditions, not being able to fend itself with adequate calories per day is something that has been a matter of agreement among all the experts and government statistics.

This poses a question about India's democratic practice. Democracy is founded on the principles of people's participation and people's well-being. Then, how is it that continued practice of democracy takes place despite continued existence of poverty? This 'puzzle' was eloquently brought to notice by Yogendra Yadav through our conversations and also through his unpublished paper 'Search for a Feasible Social Democracy' (Yadav 2011).

This puzzle can be answered only by adopting a nuanced understanding of the way democracy functions. In a sense, this puzzle is not typical only of India. It has been argued that democracies in poor societies have various constraints and preoccupations while making policy choices. India's democracy has been more concerned with transforming the pre-existing balance of social powers. This process has meant that the emphasis has been more on bringing to the forefront new elite from previously deprived social sections. Curiously, the elite coming from the deprived sections find that retaining this newly found power is not conditional upon perceptible improvement in the life conditions of their social base. Therefore, there is less incentive for them to work for economic improvement of their voters. Poverty in a generalized sense is not seen as a scandal on par with the scandal of social inequality. Simultaneously, democratic mobilization has strengthened many community loyalties and, thus, the process of individuation has not taken off in full earnest despite the march of capitalism in the sphere

167

of economic organization. The continuous reinvention of communities and incorporation of individuals into communities deflects the focus away from poverty. Finally, democracy also raises expectation and hope that things would improve. This hope (and 'enchantment' as Kaviraj [2011] calls it) makes democracy feasible despite the failure to deliver well-being.

These are, of course, tentative answers, and they do not help us run away from the central question about India's democracy. So, we can frame the fifth paradox thus: despite continued existence, India's democracy allows the high incidence of poverty, squalor, malnutrition, ill-health, and hugely inadequate access to decent education among at least a quarter of its population (by conservative estimate). While the elite's search for political power hinges on popular approval, this conditionality does not incentivize politics for addressing poverty.

In the light of these paradoxes, it is necessary to ask where India's democracy goes from here.

Whither Democracy: Democracy's Diversions

Liberal democracies have a tendency to normalize elite rule under conditions of free political competition but *limited policy choices*. Given the routineness of elections in India, it is quite possible that such a limited version of democracy under elite rule would take shape and become the normal condition of politics. In such a condition, there is a multiplicity of formal choices in terms of number of parties and number of candidates, but most of the competitors tend to adopt a more or less similar set of policies. This creates a semblance of choice—choice of rulers *without* much choice in matters of policies. 'Normal' politics underplays the fault lines in the society and brings to the forefront a consensus that tends to dominate imagination and practice. We have seen how the Nehruvian consensus predominated in the early post-Independence period and that the decade of the 2010s came close to bringing in a new consensus that was in the making since the 1990s.

While India's democracy appears poised to gain this 'normalness', it is not devoid of the experience and possibilities of 'diversions'. India's democracy has experienced and is likely to experience, in near future, at least two critical diversions.

The absence of a liberal political–social environment always keeps diverting democratic politics. Indian society is not without its own variant of tolerance, but, theoretically, tolerance is different from a liberal norm that helps consolidate democracy through the formality of freedom of expression and freedom of even nonconformism. Resulting from the lack of a strong liberal ethic, Indian politics often witnesses various vigilante actions in the name of people's anger, people's dislike, and hurt sentiments. Vigilantism feeds on both public disappointment about inability to effectively intervene in ongoing public discourse and policy processes on the one hand, and unease with different and non-conformist views, on the other. Appropriating these two, many groups take it upon themselves to protect what they believe to be the right norms and values. Such vigilantism is justified as public expression of some strong emotion and is often mistaken by its perpetrators and supporters as 'democratic' outbursts. However, to the extent indulgence towards vigilantism is a risky proposition, vigilantism and street politics constitute a recurring diversion.

Another diversion, with which Indians are too familiar, is that of populism. Between 1969 and 1972, Indira Gandhi experimented with populist politics at the all-India level. She was successful—but only for a short period. A rhetoric that everybody was against her, a claim that she wanted to work for the poor, a constant nationalist theme, complete concentration of power in her hands through a personality cult deliberately cultivated within the party, and, above all, the demagogic skill to create the category called the 'people' and to address that category by drowning all other differentiations constituted the core elements of her populist authoritarian approach. There are many instances of populist politics at the state level too: Tamil Nadu has perhaps the longest and strongest history of populist politics displayed by both the DMK and AIADMK, Maharashtra has witnessed populism of Bal Thackeray, Andhra Pradesh has had a brief populist stint when N.T. Rama Rao emerged on the political scene there, Mamata Banerjee in West Bengal conducts her politics mostly in the populist mode, and Kejriwal, too, shows a propensity to use the populist framework.

Around the Sixteenth Lok Sabha election, all-India politics came close to most of the elements that constituted Indira Gandhi's populist politics. The elements listed earlier appear to be replaying almost like déjà vu since around 2013. This second turn towards populist diversion was occasioned by a sense of crisis and failure of politics—a feeling exacerbated both by the incompetent governance of UPA–II and the populist rhetoric of the anti-corruption movement. Narendra Modi, then chief minister of Gujarat, seized the opportunity and not only won the election, but also continued with the populist political strategies since then.

Danger of Distortions

Another trajectory of democratic politics, beyond small or large diversions, consists of distortion of the logic of democracy. A community-based majoritarian under-standing of democracy constitutes such a distortion. Just as populism bases itself on raw democratic sentiment, majoritarianism, too, is situated in the appropriation of raw passions of a community. The previous chapter has already discussed this tendency experienced in India. The difference between populism and majoritarianism is that the former is somewhat easy to push back—a reversal is easier—while the latter is likely to be more durable, more difficult to reverse, and has the capacity to make an impact even when not exercising formal political power. More than a craving for a good leader, majoritarianism represents a craving among a commu-nity to assert its claims over and above those of all oth-ers by privileging its own claims as truly democratic and representative because of numerical strength and a sense of historical ownership of geographies, cultures, and norms. This craving undercuts the normative and empirical importance of diversity. In a sense, this is connected to the fourth paradox discussed earlier—regarding the handling of diversities.

Since the late 1980s, Hindu majoritarianism has been gaining ground in India. By the 2010s, the majoritarian norm had become widespread enough to acquire prestige and legitimacy. That a party upholding Hindu majoritarianism came to power in 2014 is only one part of the larger story. It is also important to note that Hindu majoritarianism is only one, and more organized and sustained, variant of majoritarianism. Regional and caste-based versions of majoritarianism have become acceptable in many parts of the country and the so-called 'secular' and non-Hindutva forces are also not averse to majoritarian arguments in regional and caste contexts. This, more than mere Hindutva, ensures a long life for majoritarianism and also indicates not just a diversion, but also a major distortion of democracy, a distortion that is theoretically legitimized on majoritarian grounds and is also popularly accepted as a natural meaning of democracy.

In Hope and Undying Optimism

In contrast to these diversions and distortions, is it possible to expect expansion and deepening of democracy? There is often a temptation among democrats to expect that democracy would bring about large-scale transformations *ipso facto*. It is necessary to take a sober view of what democracy can achieve—what it is meant to achieve. Democracy is not a 'one-pill-cures-all-ills' magic potion. So, it is unreasonable to imagine that democracy would address all social problems. Yet, democratic politics must ideally strive for two tasks. One is to bring more and more social spheres under the rubric of democratic exchange. Beyond elections and governance, democracy needs to become the normative basis for other sociocultural fields as well. Two, the democratic norm has to become more entrenched, where people's commitment to democracy is not easily unsettled by momentary attractions or momentary disappointments. This dual process of expansion and deepening of democracy is the long term challenge for democrats. This challenge can be handled by sustained practice of democratic politics in the first place, and in any case, it is a long battle that can be fought with popular support only.

After all, democracy is best at facilitating free play of alternatives and hope.

Both optimism and hope can remain alive only through the agency of the people themselves and, in that sense, the future trajectory of democracy in India is predicated on people's engagement with a lively critique of existing democratic practice, their informed interest in democratic contestations, and in the final instance, popular initiative.

Bibliography

Note: A rich body of literature is available on different dimensions of India's democratic politics. In the present bibliography, an attempt has been made to restrict the reading list to a select few readings (including those mentioned in the text) with a view to giving the reader an idea of this richness without causing intimidation by sheer quantity. The bibliography, thus, is neither exhaustive nor expected to satisfy scholarly pursuit of the subject, but only an indicative exercise. The purpose of the bibliography is to sensitize the reader to varieties of literature and to encourage delving into the readings.

Alam, Javeed. 2004. *Who Wants Democracy?* New Delhi: Orient Longman.

Alam, Sanjeer. 2009. 'Whither Muslim Politics?' *Economic and Political Weekly*, 44(39): 92–5.

Association for Democratic Reforms. Available at http://adrindia.org/.

Austin, Granville. 1972. *The Indian Constitution: Cornerstone of a Nation*. New Delhi: Oxford University Press.

Banerjee, Sumanta. 1980. *In the Wake of Naxalbari: A History of the Naxalite Movement in India*. Calcutta: Subarnarekha.

Bardhan, Pranab. 1984. *Political Economy of Development in India*. New Delhi: Oxford University Press.

Baruah, Sanjib. 1999. *India against Itself: Assam and the Politics of Nationality*. New Delhi: Oxford University Press.

————. 2010. *Ethnonationalism in India: A Reader*. New Delhi: Oxford University Press.

Byers, Terrence. (ed.). 1998. *The State, Development Planning and Liberalization in India*. New Delhi: Oxford University Press.

Chakravorty, Sanjay. 2013. *The Price of Land: Acquisition, Conflict, Consequence*. New Delhi: Oxford University Press.

Chandra, Bipan. 2003. *In the Name of Democracy: JP Movement and the Emergency*. New Delhi: Penguin Books.

Chandra, Kanchan. 2004. *Why Ethnic Parties Succeed: Patronage and Ethnic Head Counts in India*. Cambridge: Cambridge University Press.

Chasie, Charles and Sanjoy Hazarika. 2009. *The State Strikes Back: India and the Naga Insurgency*. Washington, DC: East West Centre.

Chatterjee, Partha. 2004. *Politics of the Governed: Reflections on Popular Politics in Most of the World*. Delhi: Permanent Black.

Choudhry, Sujit, Madhav Khosla, and Pratap Bhanu Mehta. 2016. *The Oxford Handbook of the Indian Constitution*. New Delhi: Oxford University Press.

Chowdhary, Rekha. 2016. *Jammu and Kashmir: Politics of Identity and Separatism*. Oxfordshire and New York: Routledge.

Corbridge, Stuart and John Harriss. 2000. *Reinventing India*. New Delhi: Oxford University Press.

Deshpande, Ashwini. 2013. *Affirmative Action in India*. New Delhi: Oxford University Press.

Deshpande, G.P. 2009. *The World of Ideas in Modern Marathi*. New Delhi: Tulika Books.

Deshpande, Rajeshwari. 2004. 'Social Movements in Crisis?' in Rajendra Vora and Suhas Palshikar (eds), *Indian Democracy: Meanings and Practices*, pp. 379–409. New Delhi: SAGE Publications.

————. 2005. 'State and Democracy in India: Strategies of Accommodation and Manipulation', Occasional Paper Series III, no. 4. Pune: University of Pune.

Frankel, Francine. 2005. *India's Political Economy, 1947–2004*, 2nd edition. New Delhi: Oxford University Press.

Frankel, Francine and M.S.A. Rao (eds). 1989/1990. *Dominance and State Power in Modern India, Decline of a Social Order*, vols 1 and 2. New Delhi: Oxford University Press.

Freedom House. 2017. Available at https://freedomhouse. org/report/fiw-2017-table-country-scores.

Galanter, Marc. 1984. *Competing Equalities: Law and the Backward Classes in India*. Berkeley: University of California Press.

Guha, Ramachandra. 2007. *India after Gandhi*. London: Picador.

Hewitt, V. 2008. *Political Mobilization and Democracy in India: States of Emergency*. Abingdon: Routledge.

Human Development Report. 2016. Available at http:// hdr.undp.org/en/composite/trends, United Nations Development Programme.

Indian Express. 2017. 'Has PM Modi's Diwali, Ramzan bhed-bhav Remark Given More Fodder to Opposition?' New Delhi, 20 February, available at http://indianexpress.com/elections/uttar-pradesh-assembly-elections-2017/narendra-modi-diwali-ramzan-bhed-bhav-remark-given-more-fodder-to-opposition-fatehpur-up-uttar-pradesh-elections/ (accessed 14 June 2017).

Jaffrelot, Christophe and Sanjay Kumar (eds). 2009. *Rise of the Plebeians? The Changing Face of Indian Legislative Assemblies*. New Delhi: Routledge.

Jaffrelot, Christophe. 2003. *India's Silent Revolution*. Delhi: Permanent Black.

——————. 2009. *Hindu Nationalism: A Reader*. Princeton: Princeton University Press.

Jayal, Niraja Gopal and Pratap Bhanu Mehta. 2010. *The Oxford Companion to Politics in India*. New Delhi: Oxford University Press.

Jodhka, Surinder. 2014. *Caste in Contemporary India*. New Delhi: Routledge.

Kapur, Devesh and Pratap Bhanu Mehta. 2005. *Public Institutions in India: Performance and Design*. New Delhi: Oxford University Press.

Kaviraj, Sudipta. 2010a. *The Imaginary Institution of India*. Ranikhet: Permanent Black.

——————. 2010b. *The Trajectories of the Indian State*. Ranikhet: Permanent Black.

——————. 2011. *The Enchantment of Democracy and India*. Ranikhet: Permanent Black.

Khilnani, Sunil. 2003. *The Idea of India*. New Delhi: Penguin Books.

Khosla, Madhav. 2012. *The Indian Constitution*. New Delhi: Oxford University Press.

Kohli, Atul. (ed.). 1991. *India's Democracy: an Analysis of Changing State-Society Relations*. New Delhi: Orient Longman.

———. 2012. *Poverty amid Plenty in the New India*. Cambridge: Cambridge University Press.

Kothari, Rajni. 1988. *State against Democracy*. Delhi: Ajanta.

Lokniti. 2015. *Democracy in India: A Citizens' Perspective, A Report by Lokniti*. Delhi: Centre for the Study of Developing Societies.

Macmillan, Alistair. 2005. *Standing at the Margins: Representation and Electoral Reservation in India*. New Delhi: Oxford University Press.

Mehta, Pratap Bhanu. 2003. *The Burden of Democracy*. New Delhi: Penguin Books.

Menon, Nivedita and Aditya Nigam. 2007. *Power and Contestation: India since 1989*. London: Zed Books.

Misra, Udayon. 2000. *The Periphery Strikes Back: Challenges to the Nation State in Assam and Nagaland*. Shimla: Indian Institute of Advanced Study.

Munshi, Indra. 2012. *The Adivasi Question: Issues of Land, Forest and Livelihood*. New Delhi: Orient BlackSwan.

Nayyar, Deepak, Rajni Kothari, and Arjun Sengupta. 1998. *Economic Development and Political Democracy: The Interaction of Economics and Politics in Independent India*. New Delhi: National Council of Applied Economic Research.

Norris, Pipa. 2011. *Democratic Deficit: Critical Citizen Revisited*. New York: Cambridge University Press.

O'Hanlon, Rosalind. 1985. *Caste, Conflict and Ideology: Mahatma Jotirao Phule and Low Caste Protest in Nineteenth-*

Century Western India. Cambridge: Cambridge University Press.

Omvedt, Gail. 1993. *Reinventing Revolution: New Social Movements and the Socialist Transition in India*. New York: East Gate, M.E. Sharpe.

Palshikar, Suhas. 2003. 'The Regional Parties and Democracy: Romantic Rendezvous or Localized Legitimation?' in Ajay K. Mehra, D.D. Khanna, and Gert W. Queck (eds), *Political Parties and Party Systems*, pp. 306–35. New Delhi: SAGE Publications.

————. 'Majoritarian Middle Ground?' *Economic and Political Weekly*, 18(December): 5426–30.

————. 2013. 'Regional and Caste Parties', in Atul Kohli and Prerna Singh (eds), *Routledge Handbook of Indian Politics*, pp. 91–104. New York: Routledge.

————. 2015. 'The BJP and Hindu Nationalism: Centrist Politic and Majoritarian Impulses', *South Asia: Journal of South Asian Studies*, 38(4): 719–35.

Palshikar, Suhas and K.C. Suri. 2014. 'India's 2014 Lok Sabha Elections: Critical Shifts in the Long Term, Caution in the Short Term', *Economic and Political Weekly*, 27 September, 49(39): 39–49.

Rudolph, Susanne Hoeber and Lloyd I. Rudolph. 1987. *In Pursuit of Laxmi: Political Economy of State in India*. Delhi: Orient Longman.

Sarangi, Asha (ed.). 2009. *Language and Politics in India*. New Delhi: Oxford University Press.

Sathe, S.P. 2002. *Judicial Activism in India: Transgressing Borders and Enforcing Limits*. New Delhi: Oxford University Press.

SDSA Team. 2008. *State of Democracy in South Asia*. New Delhi: Oxford University Press.

Shah, Ghanshyam (ed.). 2002. *Social Movements and the State*. New Delhi: SAGE Publications.

Sharma, Jyotirmaya. 2011. *Hindutva: Exploring the Idea of Hindu Nationalism*. New Delhi: Penguin Books.

Shiva, Vandana. 2014. *The Vandana Shiva Reader*. Lexington Kentucky: University Press of Kentucky.

Singh, Ujjwal Kumar. 2007. *The State, Democracy and Anti-Terror Laws in India*. New Delhi: SAGE Publications.

Stepan, Alfred, Huan Linz, and Yogendra Yadav. 2011. *Crafting State-nations: India and Other Multi-national Democracies*. Baltimore: The Johns Hopkins University.

Suri, K.C. 2005. 'Parties under Pressure: Political Parties in India since Independence', Working Paper No. 1. Delhi: Lokniti.

Suri, Sanjay. 2015. *1984: The Anti-Sikh Riots and After*. New Delhi: HarperCollins.

Tarlo, Emma. 2003. *Unsettling Memories: Narratives of the Emergency in Delhi*. Delhi: Permanent Black.

Tillin, Louise. 2013. *Remapping India: New States and Their Political Origins*. New York: Oxford University Press.

Vanaik, Achin. 1990. *The Painful Transition: Bourgeois Democracy in India*. London: Verso.

Varadarajan Siddharth (ed.). 2002. *Gujarat: Making of a Tragedy*. New Delhi: Penguin Books.

Varshney, Ashutosh. 2013. *Battles Half Won: India's Improbable Democracy*. New Delhi: Penguin Books.

Whitehead, Judith. 2010. *Development and Dispossession in the Narmada Valley*. New York and New Delhi: Pearson.

World Democracy Audit. 2001. Available at http://www.worldaudit.org/democracy.htm.

Yadav, Yogendra. 2000. 'Understanding the Second Democratic Upsurge: Trends of Bahujan Electoral Participation in the 1990s', in Francine R. Frankel, Zoya Hasan, Rajeev Bhargava, and Balveer Arora (eds), *Transforming India: Social and Political Dynamics of Democracy in India*, pp. 120–45. New Delhi: Oxford University Press.

―――――. 2011. 'Search for a Feasible Social Democracy', unpublished paper, 19–21 November, New Delhi.

Yadav, Yogendra and Suhas Palshikar. 2003. 'From Hegemony to Convergence: Party System and Electoral Politics in the Indian State, 1952–2002', *Journal of Indian School of Political Economy*, 15(1 and 2, January–June): 5–44.

―――――. 2008. 'Ten Theses on State Politics in India', *Seminar*, 591(November): 14–22.

Index

About the Author

SUHAS PALSHIKAR has taught political science at Savitribai Phule Pune University, India. He is associated with Lokniti, a research programme on comparative democracy, based at the Centre for the Study of Developing Societies, New Delhi, and is also chief editor of the journal *Studies in Indian Politics*. He has written extensively in English and Marathi on party politics and electoral politics in India.